T H E   B O O K   O F

JAPANESE
COOKING

THE BOOK OF

JAPANESE
COOKING

EMI KAZUKO

Photographed by
SIMON BUTCHER

PUBLISHED BY
SALAMANDER BOOKS LIMITED
LONDON

Published by Salamander Books Limited
129-137 York Way, London N7 9LG, United Kingdom

9 8 7 6 5 4 3 2 1

Managing Editor: Anne McDowall
Editor: Felicity Jackson
Designer: Paul Johnson
Photographer: Simon Butcher
Photographer's Assistant: Giles Stokoe
Home Economist: Oona van den Berg
Home Economist's Assistant: Becky Johnson
Stylist: Shannon Beare
Colour separation: PixelTech Pte, Singapore
Filmset: SX DTP
Printed and bound in Spain by Bookprint, S.L.

Acknowledgment:
The publishers would like to thank Meyer (UK) Ltd.
for supplying saucepans.

Notes:
All spoon measurements are level.
1 teaspoon = 5 ml spoon
1 tablespoon = 15 ml spoon

CONTENTS

INTRODUCTION

Food fashions in the West keep looking further east for inspiration and now it seems to have reached the farthest point: Japan.

Contrary to the general belief that Japanese food looks much too beautiful to eat and thus too complicated to cook, many dishes can be prepared very quickly, using almost no fat and very small amounts of fuel. This book shows you easy ways to cook authentic Japanese dishes, using ingredients that are readily available in supermarkets and oriental shops. You will see how easily you can adapt Japanese food to your daily cooking and bring true Japanese taste to your dinner table.

There are over 80 recipes, including famous sushi, soups, fish, and shellfish, chicken and meat, vegetable side dishes, rice and noodles. Each recipe is illustrated in full colour, with clear step-by-step instructions, to make Japanese cooking accessible to all.

JAPANESE FOOD

Japan was an agricultural nation for thousands of years until after the war. Houses were traditionally constructed mostly of wood, as opposed to Western houses made of stone, so wood was, and still is, a very valuable resource.

With few other fuel resources, the Japanese had to find various ways of appreciating both their agricultural produce and the plentiful supply of fish caught in the surrounding seas without burning lots of wood and charcoal. Consequently, the Japanese developed ways of eating raw or near raw food.

Eating totally raw fish may seem intimidating to the Western world but in Japan it is considered the best, if not the only, way to appreciate the real flavour of fish, and sashimi (prepared raw fish) has pride of place in a Japanese meal. Fish for sashimi must be really fresh – frozen fish cannot be used. It should be refrigerated until ready to use and handled as little as possible. To ensure freshness, Japanese restaurants often keep fish for sashimi alive in tanks until they are required.

Another Japanese speciality is sushi, based on boiled rice which is flavoured with a rice vinegar mixture while warm. It is then fanned to cool it quickly and give it a glossy sheen. There is a wide variety of sushi, such as raw fish seasoned with wasabi (hot green horseradish) and layered with or wrapped around the rice, or sushi rolls made with vegetables or fish enclosed in sushi rice, wrapped in nori seaweed, then rolled up and sliced.

Due to Shintoism, the ancient mythological religion, and later Buddhism, which was introduced from China, the Japanese remained a non-carnivorous nation until the opening up of the country to western influences towards the end of the nineteenth century.

Today, despite Japan's economic growth and the pressure from overseas governments to open up the domestic market, Japan is still largely a nation of fish and vegetable eaters. When meat is used, it is sliced thinly and normally cooked with vegetables. As a result, Japanese cooking is naturally healthy without even trying to be so.

COOKING AND SERVING

The most important part of Japanese cooking is the cutting of ingredients. The object is to cook vegetables of various shapes and textures to just the right crunchy softness so that they look very appetising and taste as good as they look. Different cuts and shapes have their own names; for example:
 Sengiri(shreds)
 Wagiri (rounds)
 Hangetsu (half-moons)
 Tanzaku (literally, poem card – oblong and thin)
 Hyoshigi (thick rectangles)
 Sainome (cubes)
 Arare (dice)
 Sasagaki (shavings)
 Hanagiri (flowers)

Cooking and Serving
Whether the food is being cooked for a formal banquet or a family meal, it is always very lightly done so that it is still crisp.

A formal Japanese banquet will start with hors d'oeuvres, clear soup and sashimi (prepared raw fish). This is followed in turn by a grilled dish, a steamed dish, a simmered dish and a deep-fried dish, all accompanied by vinegared or dressed salad, finishing the meal with boiled rice, miso soup and pickles.

There are not many dessert dishes in Japanese cuisine, probably due to the fact that as sugar is used in so many savoury dishes there is no need to supplement sugar intake. Another reason, of course, is that the vast amount of food eaten leaves little room for more by the end of the meal. Japanese cakes, which are eaten at tea time with green tea, are too sweet and heavy to eat after a meal, so fresh fruit and green tea almost always end a lengthy banquet. Warmed sake is drunk throughout the meal.

A simple traditional dinner at home will consist of soup and boiled rice with three main dishes – sashimi, a grilled dish and a simmered dish – all served at the same time.

JAPANESE UTENSILS

It is not necessary to buy any Japanese utensils if your kitchen is equipped with a good selection of Western cooking utensils, but the following items are particularly useful.

Daikon Grater
Japanese cooking uses a lot of grated daikon (mooli) and root ginger. An ordinary cheese grater would do the job but it is worth investing in a daikon grater which allows the juices from the ingredients to be captured in the curved base as they are grated.

Hashi
A pair of hashi (chopsticks) are the most useful tools for handling small pieces of food when cooking in the kitchen and they are the most elegant cutlery to eat with in the dining room. Although they are popularly known as chopsticks in the West – a nickname that originally meant 'nimble sticks' – this name is confusing, as hashi are not meant to chop anything. In Japanese cooking, food is served in properly cut sizes, so that you and your guests do not need to do any cutting at the table.

Once you master the art of using hashi you will find even the long, thick cooking hashi much better than forks for picking up and turning bacon and sausages while they are cooking.

Knives
Because cutting is so important in Japanese cooking, naturally Japanese knives are the cook's most cherished utensils. A Japanese chef's personal set of knives are his heart and soul and they move with him. While you do not need to have a set of Japanese knives, it is essential to have a good carving knife and a vegetable knife.

Makisu
This is a piece of bamboo blind the size of a table mat which is used mainly for rolling sushi. You can roll sushi with any flexible place mat of a similar texture, but if you are planning to make rolled sushis on a regular basis it is worth buying an authentic makisu (rolling mat).

Moulds
There are many shaped moulds but rectangular and flower ones are the most popular and the most useful. A rectangular mould is used to make pressed sushis, such as mackerel or smoked salmon, and the flower shaped one is for pretty pieces of sushis and hors d'oeuvres.

——JAPANESE INGREDIENTS——

Japanese cooking probably uses more varieties of both fresh and dried fish than any other country's cuisine and, fortunately, many of these are now to be found at good fishmongers and Japanese and Chinese supermarkets in the West. Due to the popularity of Chinese cooking, many Japanese vegetables are also available.

Daikon
This is a large, long white radish, also known as mooli, which is often grated and used to make sauces in Japanese cooking.

Dried Red Chillie
Called 'hawk's claw' in Japan because of its shape. Twice as hot as fresh chillie.

Ginger
Fresh root ginger, peeled and grated, is very popular in Japanese cooking. Vinegared ginger is also used a great deal. It is available in packets.

Hakusai
More commonly known as Chinese cabbage but Japanese in origin, the good thing about this vegetable is that unlike other vegetables it keeps fresh for quite a long time in the refrigerator, making it a convenient standby in an emergency. It is particularly good for making pickles.

Konbu
This is a giant seaweed called kelp which is sold in dried form at Japanese supermarkets. Full of vitamins and minerals, it is a health food best eaten simmered with other vegetables. Also used for dashi (fish stock).

Konnyaku
A jelly-like cake made from yam flour, it has no taste or nutritional value but is eaten for its texture. It is considered a good, healthy diet food as it cleans the stomach. It is available fresh in packets at Japanese supermarkets.

Mirin
This is a thick sweet rice wine which gives a very subtle sweet flavour to dishes. It is widely used at fashionable modern restaurants. If not available, sweet sherry can be substituted but reduce the amount of sugar in the dish to a half or a third.

Miso
Miso is a very salty paste made from fermented soya beans. It is used for soup and salad dressings and is also good in marinades for fish and meat. There are two basic types, an orangey-brown which is slightly sweeter and a reddish-brown one which is saltier.

Rice
Authentic Japanese rice, which is short-grain and slightly sticky, is kept for the home market. Californian medium-grain is a good substitute and Spain also produces a Japanese style rice. These rices vary in hardness, but Kaho-mai, Nishiki, Maruyu, Kokuho (Californian) and Minori (Spanish) – listed in order of hardness – are some of the popular brand names available.

Rice Vinegar
Japanese vinegar, made from rice, which has a very strong flavour. It is essential to use this for making sushi rice. You can buy it at oriental shops.

Sake
A strong rice wine which is made from fermented rice and water. Along with tea, it is Japan's most famous drink and the one most frequently served with meals, usually lukewarm.

Sansho pepper
A delicately pungent Japanese green pepper, which is not used for cooking but as a condiment at the table. It is available in bottles at oriental shops.

Shiitake Mushrooms
This is a widely used mushroom and is the best-known among the Japanese varieties in the West. They are also known as Chinese mushrooms. Larger supermarkets stock fresh shiitake nowadays and dried ones can be found at any oriental food shop. Dried ones have a stronger flavour than fresh.

Shoyu
The most important ingredient in Japanese cooking, known in the West as soy sauce though the Japanese name is shoyu. The word 'soy' is a regional dialect of southern Japan from where shoyu was first exported. Shoyu is made from soya beans, flour and water which is fermented and matured for several months.

Tofu
Also called bean curd, tofu is made from yellow soya beans and is widely used as a health food. In Japan tofu shops still make it every day and traditionally there are two kinds, silk or cotton, made from soya milk sieved through silk or cotton cloth.

You can buy fresh as well as pre-packed tofu at oriental foodshops. The fresh one available outside Japan is normally a cotton tofu and the pre-packed one is a silk tofu. There are two types of pre-packed tofu, firm and soft, but the firm one is recommended for cooking.

Wakame
Young brown seaweed with a delicate flavour and soft but crisp texture; it is normally available in cut and dried form. It is used for soups and salads.

Wasabi
Hot, green horseradish, sold in tubes or powdered form, and used with raw fish. Mix powdered wasabi with the same amount of warm water.

DASHI

10 cm (4 in) square of dried konbu (kelp)
40 g (1½ oz) hana-katsuo (dried bonito flakes)

Wipe konbu with a damp cloth, place in a saucepan with 685 ml (24 fl oz/3 cups) water and leave to soak for about 1 hour. Heat, uncovered, over medium heat for about 10 minutes, removing the konbu just before reaching boiling point so it retains its subtle flavour. If the thickest part of the konbu is still hard, return it to the pan for a few more minutes, adding a little water to prevent it boiling. Reserve the konbu.

Add 25 g (1 oz) of the hana-katsuo to the pan. Bring back to the boil (do not stir) and immediately remove from the heat. Using a tablespoon or ladle, remove the foam from surface and leave to stand for a few minutes until the hana-katsuo settles down to the bottom of pan. Strain the liquid through a sieve lined with muslin and reserve the hana-katsuo. This dashi (known as first dashi) is good for clear soups; however, for strongly flavoured soups, noodle broths and simmering, second dashi is used.

To make second dashi, put reserved konbu and hana-katsuo in a saucepan with 685 ml (24 fl oz/3 cups) water and bring to the boil. Lower the heat and simmer, uncovered, for 10-15 minutes until dashi is reduced by one third. Add the last 15 g (½ oz) hana-katsuo and remove from heat. Skim off the foam, leave to stand and strain as for first dashi.

Serves 4.

Note: For instant dashi, mix dashi-no-moto (freeze-dried dashi powder) with water.

—CLEAR SOUP WITH CHICKEN—

100 g (3½ oz) chicken breast fillet
6 teaspoons cornflour
12 mange tout (snow peas)
DASHI SOUP:
1 quantity of Dashi, opposite
1 tablespoon shoyu
½ teaspoon salt

Slice chicken breast crossways diagonally into 8 pieces and pat lightly with cornflour.

Bring a saucepan of water to the boil and drop in the chicken pieces, one at a time, so that they do not stick together. Cook for a few minutes (do not overcook), then drain in a mesh bowl or a colander. Keep them warm. Remove strings from the mange tout (snow peas), trim ends and slice diagonally. Cook in boiling water for 1-2 minutes until soft but still crunchy. Set aside.

Heat dashi and season with the shoyu and salt. Place 2 pieces of cooked chicken breast and 3 mange tout (snow peas) in each of 4 individual soup bowls. Pour hot soup over them and serve at once.

Serves 4.

— CLEAR SOUP WITH PRAWNS —

4 raw jumbo (king) prawns or 8 medium size
    prawns
3 tablespoons sake or 6 tablespoons white wine
45 g (1½ oz) dried somen (very fine) noodles
cress, to garnish
DASHI SOUP:
1 quantity of dashi, page 12
1 tablespoon shoyu
½ teaspoon salt

Make a slit lengthways along the back of
each prawn and remove the black vein-like
intestine.

Place prawns in a saucepan with the sake
and 3 tablespoons water, or with the white
wine only, and steam for 2-3 minutes.
Remove from the heat and cool down in the
saucepan. Peel the prawns, leaving the tail
shell on. Cook the noodles in boiling water
for about 3 minutes then rinse in cold water,
changing the water several times. Divide the
noodles between 4 individual soup bowls.
Place one large prawn or 2 medium size ones
on each portion of noodles.

Heat the dashi and season with the shoyu
and salt. Pour the hot soup gently over the
prawns and noodles and garnish with a few
sprigs of cress.

Serves 4.

──MISO SOUP WITH TOFU──

2 tablespoons dried wakame (seaweed)
3 tablespoons miso
125 g (4 oz) firm tofu, cut into tiny dice
1 spring onion, finely chopped
ground sansho pepper (optional)
STOCK:
450 ml (16 fl oz/2 cups) second dashi, page 12, or
    550 ml (20 fl oz/2½ cups) water and 1-2 tea-
    spoons dashi-no-moto (freeze-dried dashi powder)

First make the second dashi, following the method on page 12, or add dashi-no-moto to boiling water and stir to dissolve.

Meanwhile, soak the wakame in plenty of water for 10-15 minutes until fully opened up. Drain and cut the wakame into small pieces, if necessary.

Put the miso in a teacup and mix with a few spoonfuls of the stock. Return the stock to a low heat (do not boil) and add the diluted miso. Add the wakame and tofu to the pan and turn up the heat. Just before it reaches boiling point, add the finely chopped spring onion and immediately remove from the heat. Do not boil. Serve hot in individual soup bowls. Sprinkle with a little ground sansho pepper, if wished.

Serves 4.

——————EGG CUSTARD SOUP——————

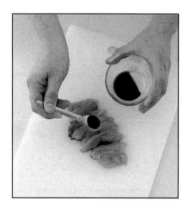

70-85 g (2½-3 oz) chicken breast, skinned
1 teaspoon each sake and shoyu
4 raw prawns, peeled and deveined
4 fresh shiitake or button mushrooms
cress, to garnish
STOCK:
450 ml (16 fl oz/2 cups) dashi, page 12 or chicken
    stock
½ teaspoon salt
1 tablespoon mirin or ½ tablespoon sugar
1 tablespoon shoyu
3 eggs, beaten

Slice chicken diagonally into small pieces; sprinkle with sake and the 1 teaspoon shoyu.

Marinate the chicken for 15 minutes, then drain. Parboil the prawns for 30 seconds and drain. Cut the stems off the mushrooms and quarter each one by slicing diagonally at the thickest part to make pieces with an even thickness. To make the stock, heat the dashi or chicken stock and season with the salt, mirin and 1 tablespoon shoyu. Allow to cool down, then gradually pour into beaten eggs, stirring gently all the time. (The mixture should not form bubbles or foam.)

Divide the prawns, chicken and mushrooms between 4 soup or tea cups and pour in egg soup until the cups are three quarters full. Cover the cups with foil. Place in a steamer and steam, covered, over low heat for 25-30 minutes. Arrange a few sprigs of cress on top, leave covered for 5 minutes, then serve hot.

Serves 4.

Variation: Cook cups in oven in a shallow baking dish half-filled with hot water at 220C(425F/Gas 7) for 25 minutes until set.

──BOILING RICE & SUMESHI──

400 g (14 oz/2 cups) Japanese rice
VINEGARY SUMESHI:
70 ml (2½ fl oz/⅓ cup) rice vinegar
1 tablespoon sugar
1 teaspoon salt

Wash the rice thoroughly, changing the water several times until it becomes clear.

Put the rice in a deep 15-18 cm (5-6 in) saucepan, with 25 per cent more cold water than rice: to do this, first cover the rice with water, then add another 1 cup of water — the water should come about 2 cm (¾ in) above the rice. Leave for 1 hour. Place the pan, covered, over high heat for 5 minutes or until you hear a sizzling noise. Reduce heat and simmer gently for 10 minutes, without lifting lid. Remove from heat and leave covered for 10 minutes. To make the sumeshi, put vinegar, sugar and salt in a jug and mix until sugar and salt have dissolved.

Transfer rice to a large bowl and gradually fold in vinegar mixture, using a wooden spatula. Do not stir. Cool the rice to room temperature using a fan; this will make it shiny. It is now ready to make sushis.

Serves 4.

Variation: To make a sweet sumeshi, add 1 tablespoon mirin to the rice cooking water. Mix 55 ml (2 oz/¼ cup) rice vinegar, 1½ tablespoons sugar and ½ teaspoon salt. Fold into the cooked rice, as above.

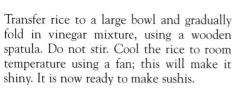

MIXED SUSHI

3-4 dried shiitake mushrooms
1½ tablespoons sugar
3½ tablespoons shoyu
½ carrot, peeled and shredded
250-350 ml (1-1½ cups) dashi, page 12
3 tablespoons sake
100 g (3½ oz) crab sticks, shredded
25 g (1 oz) french beans, trimmed
vegetable oil for frying
1 egg, beaten with a pinch of salt
VINEGARED RICE:
700 g (1½ lb/3½ cups) Japanese rice
2 tablespoons mirin
100 ml (3½ fl oz/½ cup) rice vinegar
2½ tablespoons sugar
¾ teaspoon salt

Soak the rice for vinegared rice, see page 17.
Meanwhile, soak the shiitake mushrooms in
warm water for 30 minutes, then drain,
reserving 70 ml (2½ fl oz/⅓ cup) of the water.
Discard stems and cut caps into thin strips.
Put reserved soaking water in a pan with the
sugar, 1½ tablespoons shoyu and mushroom
caps and cook for 20 minutes or until almost
all liquid is absorbed. Parboil carrot and
cook in dashi seasoned with 2 tablespoons
each shoyu and sake for 3-4 minutes.
Sprinkle remaining sake over the crab sticks.
Lightly cook beans and slice diagonally.

Heat a frying pan, pour in some vegetable
oil, then remove from heat and wipe off
excess oil. Return to medium heat and pour
in egg so that a paper-thin layer covers the
entire surface. Break air bubbles and fry both
sides for 30 seconds. Turn onto a board,
leave to cool, then cut into shreds. Make
sweet vinegared rice, see page 17; while
warm, fold in mushrooms, carrots and crab
sticks. Garnish with beans and egg shreds.

Serves 4-6.

—SUSHI IN PANCAKE PARCELS—

1-2 dried shiitake mushrooms
100 g (3½ oz) dried shrimps
3 tablespoons sake or white wine
2 tablespoons shoyu
4½ tablespoons sugar
1 sheet of nori (wafer-thin dried seaweed)
2 teaspoons sesame seeds
2 tablespoons cornflour
8 eggs, beaten
vegetable oil for frying
12-16 sprigs watercress
VINEGARED RICE:
200 g (7 oz/1 cup) Japanese rice
1 tablespoon mirin
55 ml (2 fl oz/¼ cup) rice vinegar
1½ tablespoons sugar and ½ teaspoon salt

Soak the rice for vinegared rice, see page 17. Soak mushrooms in warm water and shrimps in sake or wine for 30 minutes. Drain the mushrooms, reserving 70 ml (2½ fl oz/⅓ cup) of the water. Put the reserved water in a pan with the shoyu and 2 tablespoons sugar, add the mushrooms and cook for 10 minutes. Leave to cool, then finely chop. Meanwhile, drain the shrimps and chop roughly if large. Place nori over heat and lightly grill both sides for a second until crisp. Crumble it in absorbent kitchen paper. In a dry saucepan, toast sesame seeds and crush roughly.

Mix cornflour with 2 tablespoons water and stir into eggs with remaining 2½ tablespoons sugar. Heat a pancake pan and wipe a little oil over base. Add a little of the egg, tilting pan to spread it evenly. Cook for 30 seconds on each side. Repeat to make 12-16 very thin pancakes. Make sweet vinegared rice, see page 17, and, while warm, fold in nori, shrimps, mushrooms and sesame seeds. Wrap 2-3 tablespoonfuls of rice in a pancake, then tie up like a money bag with watercress.

Makes 12-16.

──MACKEREL SUSHI──

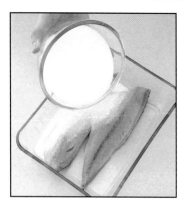

500 g (1 lb 2 oz) mackerel, filleted
salt and rice vinegar
VINEGARED RICE:
200 g (7 oz/1 cup) Japanese rice
2½ tablespoons rice vinegar
½ tablespoon sugar
½ teaspoon salt
GARNISH:
lemon wedges and cress
vinegared ginger slices, optional

Start the preparation for this dish 1-2 days beforehand. Place the mackerel fillets in a dish, cover completely with plenty of salt and leave overnight in the refrigerator.

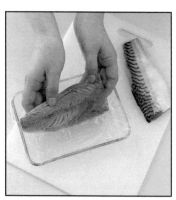

Make the vinegared rice, see page 17. Remove mackerel and rub off the salt with absorbent kitchen paper. Carefully remove all the bones with tweezers. Wash off any remaining salt with rice vinegar. Using your fingers, remove transparent skin from each fillet, leaving silver pattern on flesh intact. Place a fillet, skinned side down, in a wet wooden mould or rectangular container, about 25 x 7.5 x 5 cm (10 x 3 x 2 in), lined with a large piece of plastic wrap. Fill the gaps with small pieces taken from the other fillet so the mould is lined.

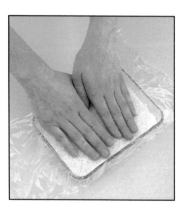

Press vinegared rice down firmly on top of the fish with fingers. Put the wet wooden lid on, or fold in the plastic wrap, and place a weight on top. Leave in a cool place (not refrigerator) for a few hours. Remove from container, unwrap, and cut into small pieces with a sharp knife, wiping the knife with a vinegar-soaked cloth or paper after each cut. Garnish with lemon, cress, and vinegared ginger slices, if wished. Serve with shoyu handed separately in small individual dishes.

Serves 4-6 as a starter.

——SMOKED SALMON SUSHI——

2 tablespoons dashi, page 12
2 tablespoons shoyu
175 g (6 oz) smoked salmon, thickly sliced
capers and lemon wedges, to garnish
VINEGARED RICE:
200 g (7 oz/1 cup) Japanese rice
2½ tablespoons rice vinegar
½ tablespoon sugar
½ teaspoon salt

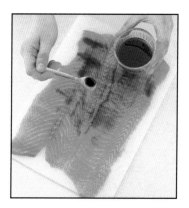

Make the vinegared rice, see page 17. Mix
the dashi and shoyu, sprinkle it over the
smoked salmon and leave to marinate for at
least 30 minutes. Drain well and pat dry.

Lay half the salmon evenly in bottom of a
wet wooden mould or rectangular container,
measuring 25 x 7.5 x 5 cm (10 x 3 x 2 in),
lined with a large piece of plastic wrap.
Using hands, firmly press down enough
vinegared rice to make a 1 cm (½ in) layer
on top. Repeat this with the rest of the
smoked salmon and sumeshi to make a 3 cm
(1¼ in) thick, double-layer sushi. Put wet
wooden lid on, or fold in plastic wrap, and
place a weight on top. Leave in a cool place
(not the refrigerator) for 2-3 hours or
overnight.

Remove from container, unwrap, and cut
into bite-size pieces, using a sharp knife to
prevent the layers separating, and wiping
the knife with a vinegar-soaked cloth or
paper after each cut. Arrange pieces on a
Japanese lacquered tray, or a large serving
plate, and garnish with some capers on top
and lemon wedges by the side. Serve on
individual plates with a little shoyu.

Serves 4-6 as a starter.

──CHERRY BLOSSOM SUSHI──

⅓ teaspoon salt
2 teaspoons sake
3 tablespoons cooked peeled small prawns
2 teaspoons sesame seeds
100 g (3½ oz) cod fillet
2 tablespoons sugar
red vegetable colouring agent
watercress sprigs, to garnish
VINEGARED RICE:
200 g (7 oz/1 cup) Japanese rice
1 tablespoon mirin
55 ml (2 fl oz/¼ cup) rice vinegar
1½ tablespoons sugar
½ teaspoon salt

Soak rice for vinegared rice, see page 17. Meanwhile, sprinkle a pinch of salt and a dash of sake over the prawns. Heat a small dry saucepan and toast the sesame seeds, then put them in a mortar and crush 2-3 times with a pestle just to bring out the flavour. Make the vinegared rice, see page 17, and, while still warm, fold in the prawns and sesame seeds. Cook the cod fillet in just enough boiling water to cover, then drain. Skin the fillet, carefully remove all the small bones. Pat dry with absorbent kitchen paper.

Using a fork, crush fish to make fine flakes. Put fish, sugar and remaining sake and salt in a pan and cook over low heat for 1 minute, stirring. Dilute a drop of colouring agent with a little water and add to pan, stirring vigorously to spread the colour evenly. Lay some pink flakes on bottom of a small flower mould and press some rice on top. Turn out on to a plate. Repeat until all the fish and rice are used. Arrange as 'cherry blossoms' on serving plates with watercress for leaves.

Serves 4-6 as a starter.

──────NORI-ROLLED SUSHI──────

6 cm (2½ in) piece cucumber
wasabi paste or powder
3 sheets of nori (wafer-thin dried seaweed)
100 g (3½ oz) fresh tuna or smoked salmon, cut
    into 0.5 cm (¼ in) strips
6 cm (2½ in) takuan (pickled daikon), cut into
    0.5 cm (¼ in) strips
vinegared ginger slices, to garnish
VINEGARED RICE:
200 g (7 oz/1 cup) Japanese rice
55 ml (2 fl oz/¼ cup) rice vinegar
1 tablespoon sugar and 1 teaspoon salt

Make the vinegared rice, see page 17, and
set aside.

Quarter cucumber lengthways, discarding
the seed part, and cut into 0.5 cm (¼ in)
thick strips. If using wasabi powder, dissolve
about 1 teaspoon in the same amount of
water in an egg cup and stir well to make a
soft, but not runny, clay-like texture. Set
aside with the cup upside down (to prevent
air getting into it). Halve the nori sheets.
Place one at a time horizontally on a makisu
(rolling mat). Using your hands, spread
about 2-3 tablespoons of the vinegared rice
on it, leaving about 1 cm (½ in) margin on
the side furthest from you.

Spread a tiny amount of wasabi paste across
the rice in the centre and place a row of half
the cucumber strips on it. Roll up the mat
from side nearest you, wrapping cucumber in
the centre. Repeat to make another roll with
remaining cucumber, then make 2 rolls
using tuna or salmon, and 2 using the
takuan, omitting wasabi in takuan rolls.
Trim ends of rolls; cut each one into 6
pieces. Arrange on a serving plate, garnish
with ginger and serve with a little shoyu on
individual plates.

THICK ROLLED SUSHI

2 extra large eggs, beaten
2 tablespoons dashi, page 12
2 teaspoons sake and ⅓ teaspoon salt
5 tablespoons sugar
4-5 dried shiitake mushrooms
2 tablespoons shoyu
150 g (5 oz) cod fillet
red vegetable colouring agent
⅓ cucumber, shredded
4 sheets of nori (wafer-thin dried seaweed)
VINEGARED RICE:
500 g (1 lb 2 oz/2½ cups) Japanese rice
55 ml (2 oz/¼ cup) rice vinegar
2⅓ teaspoons sugar
⅓ teaspoon salt

Make vinegared rice, see page 17, and set aside. In a small pan, make a firm omelette using the eggs mixed with the dashi, sake, salt and 2½ tablespoons sugar, see page 26, and cut into 0.5 cm (¼ in) thick strips. Soak the dried shiitake mushrooms in warm water for 30 minutes, then drain, reserving 70 ml (2½ fl oz/⅓ cup) of soaking water. Trim stems off and cut mushrooms into thin strips. Place in a pan with reserved soaking water, shoyu and remaining sugar; cook for 10 minutes. Cook the cod and make pink cod flakes, see Cherry Blossom Sushi, page 22.

Place one nori sheet vertically on a makisu (rolling mat). Spread one quarter of the rice evenly over it, leaving 1 cm (½ in) margin at furthest side. Put one strip each of all the ingredients across centre of rice and roll up from side nearest you. Keeping end of the nori down, press firmly into a round shape. Repeat to make 3 more rolls. Leave to settle for at least 30 minutes, then cut each roll into 6. Arrange on a serving plate and serve with a little shoyu in individual dishes.

Makes 24 pieces.

——HAND-ROLLED SUSHI——

700 g (1½ lb/3½ cups) Japanese rice
4-5 dried shiitake mushrooms
2½ tablespoons sugar
1 tablespoon mirin
2 tablespoons shoyu, plus extra for dipping
225 g (8 oz) fresh tuna
115 g (4 oz) smoked salmon
8 raw jumbo (king) prawns
1 avocado
⅓ cucumber, shredded
1 punnet of cress
8 sheets of nori (wafer-thin dried seaweed)

Soak the Japanese rice as for vinegared rice, see page 17.

Meanwhile, soak the shiitake mushrooms in warm water for 30 minutes then drain, reserving 70 ml (2½ fl oz/⅓ cup) of soaking water. Trim the stems off and cut the caps into thin strips. Place in a pan with the sugar, mirin, 2 tablespoons shoyu and the reserved soaking water; cook for 10 minutes. Slice the tuna into 5 x 1 cm (2 x ½ in) thin pieces. Cut the smoked salmon into similar sized slices. Peel, de-vein and lightly boil the prawns. Drain and slice horizontally in half. Peel, stone and thinly slice the avocado.

Boil rice, see page 17, and divide between 4 individual serving bowls with lids on to keep rice warm. On a large serving plate, arrange all the prepared ingredients and place it in the centre of the table. Lightly grill both sides of nori sheets over low heat and cut each one into 4 squares so that each diner has 8 small sheets. At the table, take one sheet in your palm, put in a little boiled rice spreading it with a spatula or fork. Wrap any ingredients in it, dip in shoyu and eat.

Serves 4.

ROLLED OMELETTE

100 ml (3½ fl oz/½ cup) warm dashi, page 12, or
  chicken stock
⅓ teaspoon salt
2 teaspoons mirin or 1 teaspoon sugar
⅔ tablespoon shoyu
6 eggs, lightly beaten
vegetable oil for frying
grated daikon (mooli), to garnish

Mix the warm stock, salt, mirin or sugar, and shoyu in a bowl and gently stir in the beaten eggs. Place a large frying pan over moderate heat and wipe base with vegetable oil, using a cloth or absorbent kitchen paper.

When the pan is just hot, pour one third of the mixture into the pan and tilt to spread it evenly over base. Break the air bubbles with a fork. When the egg is nearly hard, fold about 2.5 cm (1 in) from left and right sides in towards the centre to make an oblong shape then, with hashis or spatula, roll the egg layer towards you. Using the oily cloth or kitchen paper, oil the empty part of the pan, push the just-rolled egg to the other side and complete the oiling of the base. Keeping the egg roll at the other end, pour half of the remaining mixture into the pan.

Tilt pan to spread mixture evenly and allow it to run beneath egg roll. When the second layer starts to set, repeat the rolling using the first roll as the core. Without removing the roll from the pan, repeat once more with remaining egg. Turn out onto a makisu (rolling mat) and wrap tightly. Some juice should run out if omelette is not overdone. Leave to settle for a few minutes, then unwrap and cut into 4. Serve on individual plates, garnished with daikon and shoyu.

Serves 4.

EGG TOFU

500 ml (20 fl oz/2½ cups) dashi, page 12, or
   chicken stock
1 tablespoon salt
3 tablespoons each mirin and shoyu
6 eggs, well beaten but not frothy
finely sliced rind from ½ lemon, to garnish
hana-katsuo (dried bonito flakes), to serve
SAUCE:
200 ml (7 fl oz/1 cup) dashi
3 tablespoons mirin
3 tablespoons shoyu

Line the base and 2 of the sides of a 20 cm
(8 in) square baking dish with a sheet of foil,
allowing excess foil to hang over the sides.

In a bowl, mix the dashi or chicken stock,
salt, mirin and shoyu and stir in beaten eggs.
Pour the mixture into the lined dish and
steam in a steamer for 3 minutes. Lower the
heat and continue steaming for a further 25
minutes. Remove dish from the steamer and
run a knife along the unlined sides. Lift out
egg tofu, holding the 2 hanging ends of the
foil, and place it on a cutting board.

Cut egg tofu into 8 cakes and place 2 cakes
in each of 4 deep individual dishes. In a
saucepan, mix the sauce ingredients and
bring to the boil. Remove from heat and
gently pour sauce over the egg tofu cakes.
Arrange sliced lemon rind and hana-katsuo
on top and serve. To serve cold, chill the
tofu and sauce separately.

Serves 4.

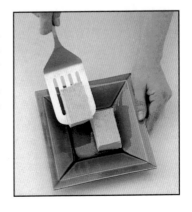

—FRIED TOFU IN DASHI SAUCE—

10 cm (4 in) piece large daikon (mooli), peeled
1 dried or fresh red chilli, deseeded
500 g (1 lb 2 oz) (2 cakes) firm tofu
plain flour for coating
vegetable oil for deep frying
SAUCE:
200 ml (7 fl oz/1 cup) dashi, page 12
2½ tablespoons shoyu
2 tablespoons mirin

Poke a chopstick into the daikon to make a few holes lengthways. Push in red chilli strips; if using a fresh chilli, make one large hole in centre of daikon by screwing in a peeler. Grate to make rust-coloured daikon.

Combine sauce ingredients in a saucepan, heat and keep warm. Quarter each tofu cake, roll in the flour and pat off excess. Heat the oil in a deep-fat fryer to 180C (350F) and fry the tofu pieces, 4 at a time, for about 8 minutes or until lightly golden, turning 2-3 times. Remove from the oil and drain on absorbent kitchen paper.

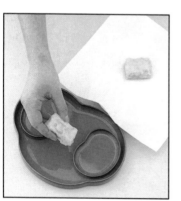

Arrange the fried tofu pieces, 2 at a time in individual dishes, on decorative absorbent kitchen paper if liked. Serve accompanied by other smaller dishes for the dipping sauce. Serve the hot sauce in a gravy boat and the daikon relish in a bowl so that diners can mix the two to make their own sauce.

Serves 4.

Note: This rust-coloured grated daikon, known as momiji-orishi (autumn maple leaf relish) is best grated with a daikon grater.

-FRIED TOFU WITH VEGETABLES-

500 g (1 lb 2 oz) (2 cakes) tofu
vegetable oil for deep frying
10 Chinese cabbage leaves (hakusai)
100 g (3½ oz) spinach
200 ml (7 oz/1 cup) dashi, page 12
2 tablespoons shoyu
1 tablespoon sugar

Parboil tofu for 3-5 minutes, drain and pat dry. Heat oil in a frying pan over high heat and add tofu cakes, one at a time. Deep-fry for a few minutes or until golden brown all over, turning 2-3 times. Remove from pan, drain and cool on absorbent kitchen paper.

Parboil cabbage leaves for a few minutes and cut into 5 cm (2 in) strips. Roughly chop the spinach. Halve deep-fried tofu lengthways and then cut into 0.5 cm (¼ in) thick slices. Heat the dashi over moderate heat and add the cabbage, shoyu and sugar. Stir well, then add the spinach and fried tofu slices. Simmer for 1-2 minutes. Check the seasoning, then remove from heat.

In 4 deep individual dishes, arrange some cabbage, then put spinach and fried tofu on top and pour over the simmering soup. Serve immediately.

Serves 4.

GRILLED TOFU WITH MISO SAUCE

500 g (1 lb 2 oz) (2 cakes) firm cotton tofu
toasted sesame seeds for sprinkling
bamboo leaves, to garnish
MISO SAUCE:
100 g (3½ oz) miso
1 egg yolk
1 tablespoon each sake, mirin and sugar
4 tablespoons dashi, page 12
juice of ¼ lime

Wrap each tofu cake in a tea towel and place a light weight, such as a plate, on top to squeeze out the water. Leave to stand for at least 1 hour.

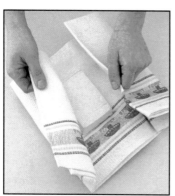

To make sauce, put the miso in a bowl and blend in the egg yolk, sake, mirin and sugar. Place bowl over a saucepan of simmering water. Gradually add the dashi and stir until sauce becomes thick but not too hard, then add the lime juice. Remove from the heat immediately and cool to room temperature (it will keep well in the refrigerator, if wished.)

Preheat grill. Unwrap the tofu cakes and cut into 5 x 2 x 1 cm (2 x ¾ x ½ in) slices. Skewer each of the slices lengthways with 2 bamboo skewers. Grill them under high heat for a few minutes on each side until lightly browned and heated through. Remove from heat and, using a butter knife, thickly spread one side with miso sauce. Sprinkle with the toasted sesame seeds. Grill miso-covered side for 1-2 minutes. Serve hot on skewers on a bed of bamboo leaves.

Serves 4 as a starter.

CUCUMBER IN VINEGAR DRESSING

10 g (2 sachets) cut dried wakame
1 cucumber
1 teapoon salt
fresh root ginger, peeled and shredded, to garnish
VINEGAR DRESSING:
4 tablespoons rice vinegar
1 tablespoon shoyu
½ tablespoon sugar

Soak the wakame in tepid water for 5-15 minutes, or according to packet instructions, until fully expanded. Halve the cucumber lengthways and, using a tablespoon, roughly scoop out seeds.

Slice cucumber halves very thinly to make half-moons and spread out on a cutting board. Sprinkle them with the salt and squash with your hand a few times. Using both hands, squeeze out the water, then put cucumber in a mixing bowl. Do not wash. Drain the wakame and plunge in boiling water for 1 minute. Drain and place under cold running water to cool down. Trim off any hard parts, then chop into bite-size pieces. Pat dry with absorbent kitchen paper and put in the mixing bowl with cucumber.

Mix the vinegar, shoyu and sugar, stirring well until the sugar has dissolved. Pour into the mixing bowl and gently mix to fold the dressing into the cucumber and wakame. Arrange in a heap in the centre of a shallow dish or in a salad bowl, garnish with finely shredded ginger and serve.

Serves 4.

—CHINESE LEAVES & KIMCHEE—

20 Chinese cabbage leaves (hakusai)
1-2 fresh red or green chillies, deseeded
2 teaspoons salt
2 tablespoons kimchee dressing (Korean chilli and
   garlic dressing)
finely shredded lemon rind, to garnish

Wash and trim the Chinese cabbage leaves. Cut in half lengthways, then crossways into 5 cm (2 in) pieces. Chop the chilli into fine half-rings.

Put a quarter of the Chinese leaves in a freezer bag and sprinkle with one quarter of the salt and chilli. Add another quarter of the leaves on top and sprinkle with another quarter of the salt and chilli. Repeat this two more times with the remaining ingredients and shake the bag to spread the salt and chilli pieces evenly throughout the leaves. Tie the bag almost air-tight and leave in the refrigerator for at least 1-2 days, preferably 1 week.

Keeping leaves in the bag, squeeze out the water, then turn out cabbage into a mixing bowl. Add kimchee dressing, mix well and arrange on a serving dish. Garnish with the shredded lemon rind and serve.

Serves 4-8.

Note: Kimchee dressing is available in jars at oriental shops.

——RADISH CHERRY BLOSSOM——

200 g (7 oz) red radishes
4 small turnips, peeled
1 teaspoon salt
200 ml (7 fl oz/1 cup) rice vinegar
150 g (5 oz/²⁄₃ cup) sugar
watercress and pomegranate seeds, to garnish

Cut the stem part off the radishes and trim the turnips so that each will stand upright. Lay a pair of cheap chopsticks, or pencils, sideways in parallel on a cutting board and place a radish in between.

Using a sharp knife, carefully make 4-6 cuts downways in the radish until the blade touches the chopsticks or pencils, so that the radish is not cut quite through. Turn the radish 90 degrees and make a few more cuts across the cuts already made. Repeat this with all the remaining radishes and also with the turnips which need far more cuts because of the size. Divide the turnips into 4-6 wedges. Put all together in a large bowl, sprinkle with the salt and lightly rub in. Cover with a small plate, place a weight on it and leave for 30 minutes.

Mix rice vinegar and sugar, stirring until the sugar has dissolved. Drain vegetables and pour the sauce over them. Leave to marinate overnight. The red colour of the radishes will melt into sauce and make turnips cherry pink as well as the radishes. Divide the pink 'cherry blossoms' between 4 individual black lacquer trays or large plates. Arrange turnips as 'petals', and watercress as 'leaves on twigs' around the 'flowers'. Arrange pomegranate seeds to look like 'fallen petals' underneath.

Serves 4.

NAMASU SALAD

15 cm (6 in) piece daikon (mooli), peeled
1-2 carrots
1 teaspoon salt
70 ml (2½ fl oz/⅓ cup) rice vinegar
3 tablespoons sugar
finely shredded lime rind, to garnish

Cut the daikon and the carrots into three 5 cm (2 in) pieces and slice each piece very thinly lengthways and then shred into thin matchsticks.

Place the matchsticks in a mixing bowl and sprinkle them with the salt. Using your hand, gently squash them, then leave for 15-20 minutes. Lightly squeeze out the water between your hands (do not press too hard) and put in another mixing bowl.

Mix rice vinegar and sugar and stir well until the sugar has dissolved. Pour the mixture into daikon and carrot shreds and gently fold in to mix the 2 colours evenly. Heap it on a serving dish and garnish with finely shredded lime rind. The Japanese regard the combination of red and white as celebration colours, so this dish is considered essential for a New Year's Day brunch table.

Serves 4.

──FRENCH BEANS KINPIRA──

225 g (8 oz) french beans, trimmed, or 3 carrots
    or parsnips, peeled
1 dried or fresh red chilli
2 tablespoons vegetable oil
2 tablespoons sake
2 tablespoons shoyu
1 tablespoon sugar

Cut the french beans diagonally into thin
strips. If using carrots or parsnips, cut them
into 5 cm (2 in) pieces, slicing lengthways
and then cut into strips.

If using dried chilli, soak it in warm water for
10-15 minutes until the outer skin is soft
enough to handle. To deseed fresh or dried
chilli, cut it lengthways and scrape out the
seeds with the back of the knife blade. Chop
the chilli very finely.

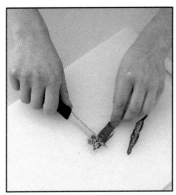

Heat a wok or a large frying pan, add the oil
and tilt the pan to spread it over the base.
Stir in the chilli and french bean, or carrot
or parsnip, strips and stir-fry over high heat
for about 3 minutes until the vegetable strips
begin to soften. Lower heat and sprinkle
with the sake, shoyu and sugar. Stir-fry over
moderate heat until the liquid is almost
completely absorbed. Serve hot or at room
temperature in one deep serving dish or in
small, deep individual dishes.

Serves 4.

—SPINACH & SESAME DRESSING—

450 g (1 lb) spinach, stemmed, or 200 g (7 oz)
   french beans, trimmed
SESAME (GOMA-AE) DRESSING:
5 tablespoons white sesame seeds
1½ teaspoons sugar
3 teaspoons shoyu
3 tablespoons dashi, page 12

Prepare the dressing first. Heat a small dry
saucepan and toast the sesame seeds.

Remove from the heat and transfer the seeds
to a large suribachi (Japanese grinding bowl)
or mortar. Crush and grind the seeds with a
pestle until they form a paste. Add the sugar,
shoyu and dashi to the mortar and blend
vigorously to make a fairly smooth dressing.

Cook the spinach in lightly salted boiling
water for about 1 minute, then drain and
immediately rinse under cold running water
to cool it quickly and preserve the bright
green colour. Lightly squeeze out the water
and chop roughly into 3 cm (1¼ in) pieces.
(If using french beans, cook them for a few
minutes until tender, then cut diagonally
into thin strips.) Add the dressing to the
spinach, or beans, and gently fold in. Serve
heaped in small deep dishes.

Serves 4.

─────── TRICOLOUR SALAD ───────

1 carrot
8 cm (3½ in) piece large daikon (mooli), peeled
salt
150 g (5 oz) mange tout (snow peas), trimmed
DRESSING:
1 tablespoon shoyu
3 tablespoons vegetable oil
2 tablespoons rice vinegar
⅓ teaspoon salt
freshly ground black pepper

Chop the carrot and daikon separately into 4 cm (1½ in) shreds. Put them in 2 large mixing bowls and sprinkle each with a pinch of salt. Leave for 15 minutes.

Cook the mange tout (snow peas) in salted boiling water for 1-2 minutes until tender but still crisp. Drain and immediately rinse under cold running water. Slice each mange tout slightly diagonally into 3 pieces. Arrange the different vegetable shreds on a serving dish, each occupying one third of the dish.

In a bowl, mix the shoyu, oil and vinegar. Add the salt and a pinch of pepper. Blend vigorously with a whisk and pour into a serving bowl or a gravy boat. The vegetables and the dressing are served separately and mixed together at the table before eating.

Serves 4.

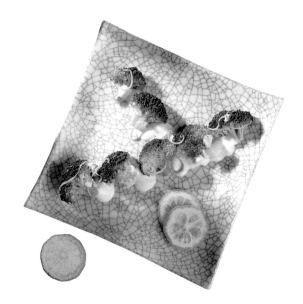

-BROCCOLI WITH MAYONNAISE-

600 g (1⅓ lb) broccoli, trimmed
DRESSING:
½ lemon
6 tablespoons mayonnaise
juice of 1 lime

First make the dressing. Cut 2-3 thin slices from the lemon half and finely shred the rind from remainder. Put the mayonnaise in a small mixing bowl and stir in the lime juice and half of the shredded lemon rind.

Make a cross slit on the bottom of the remaining stems of the broccoli so that the stems will cook as quickly as the green parts. Put the broccoli, head down, in a deep saucepan of salted boiling water and boil gently for 2-3 minutes, turning a few times. Drain and separate into small sections.

Arrange the broccoli on a serving dish or individual plates and pour the mayonnaise over it. Sprinkle the remaining lemon rind on top and garnish with lemon slices. Serve at once.

Serves 4.

Note: Lemon rind is preferable to lime rind in this dish because of the colour as well as the flavour.

─────GRILLED AUBERGINE─────

4 aubergines (eggplants), stemmed
vegetable oil for frying
GINGER SAUCE:
70 ml (2½ fl oz/⅓ cup) dashi, page 12
2 tablespoons shoyu
2 tablespoons mirin or 2 teaspoons sugar
2 tablespoons sake
4-5 cm (1½-2 in) piece fresh root ginger, peeled
8 fresh mint leaves
SESAME SAUCE:
3 tablespoons white sesame seeds
3 tablespoons dashi
1½ tablespoons shoyu
½ tablespoon sugar
salt

To make ginger sauce, put the dashi, shoyu, mirin or sugar and sake in a saucepan and boil for 1 minute. Remove from heat and set aside. Grate ginger with a Japanese daikon grater or a cheese grater. Finely shred mint leaves. To make sesame sauce, toast sesame seeds in a small dry saucepan, then grind them to a paste in a suribachi (Japanese grinding bowl) or a mortar. Mix in the dashi and shoyu. Season with sugar and a pinch of salt. Slice aubergines (eggplants) lengthways into quarters and fry, in batches, in a little oil over high heat for 1-2 minutes on each side.

Place 2 slices on each of 8 small plates. Arrange the grated ginger and mint slices on top of 4 of the plates and add the ginger sauce. Pour the sesame sauce over the aubergine slices on the other 4 plates. Serve one of each type to each person.

Serves 4.

Note: This dish is also excellent cooked on a barbecue.

VEGETABLE TEMPURA

1 carrot
1 turnip or parsnip
200 g (7 oz) french beans, trimmed
vegetable oil for deep-frying
½ daikon (mooli), peeled and grated
4-5 cm (1½-2 in) piece fresh root ginger, peeled
    and grated
lemon wedges, to garnish
BATTER:
1 egg yolk
200 ml (7 fl oz/1 cup) ice cold water
200 g (7 oz/1 cup) plain flour, sifted
SAUCE:
200 ml (7 fl oz/1 cup) dashi, page 12
70 ml (2½ oz/⅓ cup) each shoyu and mirin

Cut carrot and turnip into 5 cm (2 in) long
shreds. Cut beans diagonally into fine strips.
Heat plenty of oil in a wok or deep frying
pan to 170C (340F). Meanwhile, make the
batter. In a large mixing bowl, lightly beat
the egg and pour in the ice cold water. Stir
just 2-3 times, then add the flour. Using 3 or
4 chopsticks or a fork, very lightly mix the
batter with just a few strokes. Do not whisk
or overmix – the batter should be very
lumpy. Put all the vegetable shreds into the
bowl and gently fold in.

Carefully drop a tablespoonful at a time of
battered vegetables into the oil. Fry a few at
a time and remove from the oil when both
sides are light golden and drain on absorbent
kitchen paper. Repeat until all the battered
vegetables are cooked. Arrange them on a
large serving plate or individual plates with
heaps of grated daikon and ginger. Garnish
with lemon wedges. Quickly heat the dashi,
shoyu and mirin in a pan and pour it into
small individual bowls. Serve hot.

Serves 4.

——CRAB STICK DAIKON ROLL——

10 cm (4 in) square of dried konbu (kelp)
1 large daikon (mooli), peeled
200 g (7 oz) crab sticks
4 cm (1½ in) piece fresh root ginger, peeled and
    cut into matchsticks
watercress, to garnish
DRESSING:
2 dried or fresh red chillies
8 tablespoons dashi, page 12
4 tablespoons rice vinegar
3 tablespoons sugar
salt and 2-3 teaspoons vegetable oil

Slice daikon into 2.5 mm (¹⁄₁₀ in) rounds and spread out on a wire rack. Dry for 24 hours.

The next day, soak the konbu in warm water for 10 minutes, then cut it lengthways into 0.3 cm (⅛ in) strings. Divide each crab stick lengthways into 2-3 pieces. Place a piece of crab stick and 1-2 shreds of ginger on a dried and softened piece of daikon and roll up. Tie with a string of konbu so that it won't open up. Repeat for the remaining ingredients. Put all the rolls in a mesh bowl or colander and pour over boiling hot water. Drain and set aside.

If using dried chillies, soak in warm water for 10 minutes. Whether using dried or fresh, cut in half lengthways and remove the seeds, then slice diagonally into thin strips. Put the dashi, rice vinegar, sugar, a little salt and oil in a saucepan and bring to the boil. Stir to dissolve sugar and add chilli strips. Boil for a few seconds and remove from heat. Leave to cool. Place daikon rolls in a bowl, pour over dressing and marinate overnight. Transfer to a serving dish and garnish with watercress.

Serves 4-8 as an hors d'oeuvre.

—BABY CLAMS WITH MUSTARD—

400 g (14 oz) spinach, trimmed
a little shoyu
300 g (10 oz) canned baby clams
sake or white wine and salt
DRESSING:
1 teaspoon mustard
2 tablespoons shoyu
1 tablespoon sake or white wine
1 tablespoon rice vinegar
⅓ teaspoon salt

Cook the spinach in salted boiling water for
1-2 minutes and drain. Lightly squeeze the
water out with your hands and cut the
spinach into 5 cm (2 in) long pieces.

Put the spinach in a mixing bowl, sprinkle
with a little shoyu and set aside. Drain the
baby clams and pour boiling water over
them. Drain well and sprinkle with a dash of
sake or wine and salt. To make dressing, mix
the mustard, shoyu, sake or wine, rice vinegar and salt. Stir well until the mustard has
dissolved, then transfer the dressing to a
small serving bowl or a ramekin.

Arrange the baby clams on a bed of spinach
on a serving plate. Serve with the dressing
on the side.

Serves 4 as a starter.

—SQUID & CUCUMBER SALAD—

500 g (1 lb 2 oz) squid, cleaned
½ cucumber
salt
DRESSING:
1 teaspoon mustard
2 tablespoons shoyu
1 teaspoon sake
1 teaspoon sesame oil

Peel the outer skin off the squid, then cut squid in half lengthways. Wash inside well and parboil, with the tentacles, for 1 minute. Drain and immediately rinse under cold running water to stop further cooking.

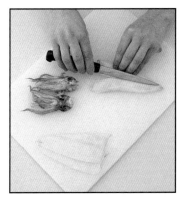

Cut the body parts in half lengthways and then crossways into 0.5 cm (¼ in) strips. Separate the tentacles and chop each into 4-5 cm (1½-2 in) pieces. Put the squid in a large mixing bowl.

Halve the cucumber lengthways. Using a tablespoon, scoop out the seeds. Slice the cucumber into thin half-moons and sprinkle with a pinch of salt. Lightly squash with a hand to squeeze out the water, then add to the squid in the bowl. In a small cup, mix all the ingredients for the dressing and pour into the squid and cucumber mixture. Toss the squid and cucumber in the dressing and serve in small individual dishes.

Serves 4 as a starter.

–SASHIMI WITH WASABI SAUCE–

1 small octopus and salt
700 g (1½ lb) very fresh Dover or lemon sole,
   filleted
lemon wedges and cress, to garnish
WASABI SAUCE:
juice of ½ lemon
1½ tablespoons shoyu
½ tablespoon olive oil
1½ teaspoons wasabi paste or powder

Separate the octopus tentacles and clean out the suckers, using a brush, and the body. Put in lightly salted boiling water and cook over moderate heat for 5-6 minutes. Drain and leave to cool slowly.

Carefully remove all the small bones from the sole. If filleted into 2 fillets, halve both lengthways. Place a quarter sole fillet on a cutting board with the skin side down and insert the blade between the skin and the flesh at the tail-end. Firmly holding the tail end, run the blade carefully along the skin towards the head end to separate the flesh. Repeat this skinning for the remaining fillets and slice crossways into 1.5 cm (⅔ in) thick pieces, inserting the blade diagonally in line with the pattern of the fish flesh.

Chill octopus in the refrigerator, then slice tentacles and body into 0.5 cm (¼ in) thick rings, cutting diagonally. Mix all the sauce ingredients with 1 tablespoon water (if using powdered wasabi, mix it with a little warm water to form a paste before mixing with remaining sauce ingredients.) Arrange sole around edge of a large serving plate and heap octopus discs in centre. Pour over half the sauce. Garnish with lemon and cress and serve accompanied by the rest of the sauce.

Serves 4-8 as an hors d'oeuvre.

──SEA BASS HAKATA-OSHI──

500 g (1 lb 2 oz) very fresh sea bass, filleted and
   skinned
salt
115 ml (4 floz/½ cup) rice vinegar
½ cucumber
4 cm (1½ in) piece fresh root ginger
2-3 basil leaves, chopped
lime slices, to garnish
VINEGAR DRESSING:
4 tablespoons each rice vinegar and dashi, page 12
2 tablespoons shoyu
½ tablespoon sugar

Remove all small bones from fillets and slice
horizontally into 1 cm (½ in) thick fillets.

Sprinkle with a pinch of salt and leave for
5 minutes. Pat dry and marinate in the rice
vinegar for a few minutes. Meanwhile, slice
the cucumber very thinly lengthways and
soak in salted water for about 10 minutes
until soft, then drain. Peel and cut the root
ginger into very thin matchsticks. Mix all
the ingredients for the vinegar dressing in a
pan and simmer over moderate heat for a
few minutes until the sugar has dissolved.
Remove from the heat and leave to cool.

Place a large sheet of plastic wrap on a
cutting board and lay half the sea bass slices
in the centre. Spread the ginger shreds and
then the cucumber slices evenly on top and
sprinkle with the chopped basil leaves.
Cover with the remaining sea bass and wrap
with the plastic wrap. Put another board on
top and press for a few minutes. Unwrap and
cut into 5 x 2.5 cm (2 x 1 in) pieces. Arrange
in individual dishes and garnish with lime
slices. Serve with small bowls of dressing.

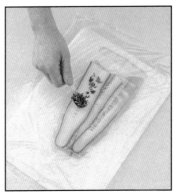

Serves 4.

TEMPURA

4 raw king (jumbo) or 8 medium prawns
350-400 g (12-14 oz) whiting fillets
plain flour for coating
4-8 fresh shiitake or button mushrooms
8 asparagus tips or okra
vegetable oil for deep-frying
grated daikon (mooli) and fresh root ginger,
    to garnish
BATTER:
1 egg yolk, beaten
200 ml (7 fl oz/1 cup) ice cold water
200 g (7 oz/1 cup) plain flour, sifted
DIPPING SAUCE:
200 ml (7 fl oz/1 cup) dashi, page 12
55 ml (2 fl oz/¼ cup) mirin
70 ml (2½ fl oz/⅓ cup) shoyu

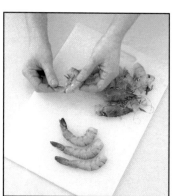

Peel the prawns, retaining the tail shell, and de-vein. Make a few slits along the belly to prevent curling during cooking. Cut the whiting fillets into pieces about 5 cm (2 in) long and roll in plain flour. If the mushrooms are large cut them in half. Heat the oil for deep-frying to 170C (340F). Meanwhile, prepare the batter: lightly mix the egg yolk with the ice cold water and add the plain flour at once. Using chopsticks or a fork, very lightly fold in the flour with just 4-5 strokes. The batter should be loosely mixed but still very lumpy.

Deep-fry asparagus tips or okra without any batter for 2-3 minutes, then drain on a wire rack. Dip mushrooms, prawns (one at a time, holding by tail) and whiting fillets in batter. Deep-fry one at a time in this order for 1-3 minutes until light golden. Drain them on the rack, then arrange one quarter of each on absorbent kitchen paper on individual plates. Boil the dashi, mirin and shoyu in a pan and pour into small individual bowls. Serve garnished with daikon and ginger.

Serves 4.

————FRIED KING PRAWNS————

16 raw king (jumbo) prawns
salt and sake
55 g (2 oz) rice vermicelli
vegetable oil for deep-frying
plain flour for coating
2 egg whites, lightly beaten
70 g (2½ oz/½ cup) dried breadcrumbs
lettuce leaves, to serve
lemon wedges, to garnish

Peel the prawns, retaining the tail shell, and de-vein. Make a few slits along the belly to prevent curling during cooking. Sprinkle with salt and a little sake and set aside.

Put the vermicelli in a bag and crush into pieces. Heat oil in a wok or deep frying pan to about 170C (340F). Holding the tail to avoid coating the tail shell, dust a prawn with flour, coat with egg white and then with breadcrumbs. Deep-fry for 2-3 minutes until golden brown, turning frequently. Drain on a wire rack. Repeat with another 7 of the prawns.

Dust the remaining 8 prawns with flour, coat with egg white and then dredge in crushed vermicelli instead of breadcrumbs. Lower the oil temperature to 160C (320F) – this lower temperature helps retain whiteness of the vermicelli. Deep-fry the prawns for 2-3 minutes, then drain on the wire rack. Arrange 2 of each type of prawn on a bed of lettuce leaves on each of 4 individual plates, garnish with lemon wedges and serve.

Serves 4.

FRIED PLAICE

1 large plaice, filleted
sake
4 tablespoons cornflour
oil for deep-frying
juice of ½ lemon
1½ tablespoons shoyu
2 tablespoons grated chile-daikon mixture, page 28

Cut plaice fillets in half lengthways and then into 5 cm (2 in) pieces. Sprinkle with a dash of sake and set aside.

Dredge the plaice pieces in the cornflour, shaking off any excess. Heat the oil in a wok or a deep frying pan to 160C (320F). Meanwhile, in a small bowl, mix the lemon juice and the shoyu to make a dipping sauce.

Deep-fry the plaice pieces for 5 minutes. Increase the heat to raise the temperature of the oil to 170C (340F) and continue frying for 2 minutes to make the fries crispy. Drain on a wire rack. Serve the fried plaice pieces with small individual bowls of the sauce, accompanied by the grated daikon relish in a small bowl.

Serves 4.

──MACKEREL TATSUTA FRY──

700 g (1½ lb) mackerel, filleted
115 g (4 oz/1 cup) cornflour
vegetable oil for deep-frying
lemon wedges, to garnish
MARINADE:
4 tablespoons sake
2 tablespoons shoyu
2.5 cm (1 in) piece fresh root ginger, peeled and
    grated

Remove the large bones from the mackerel
fillets. Slice the fillets crossways into bite-
size pieces, inserting the blade diagonally.

In a mixing bowl, combine the ingredients
for the marinade. Add mackerel pieces,
turning to coat with the marinade, then
leave to marinate for 30 minutes. Drain and
toss the mackerel in the cornflour to dust
thoroughly.

Heat oil in a wok or a deep frying pan to
160C (320F). Slide the mackerel pieces into
the hot oil, a few pieces at a time, and fry for
2-3 minutes until golden brown, turning 2-3
times. Remove from the oil and drain on a
wire rack. Arrange a quarter of the fried
mackerel on each of 4 individual plates, on
folded absorbent kitchen paper if wished.
Alternatively, heap all the fish in the centre
of a bamboo basket tray. Garnish with
lemon wedges and serve at once.

Serves 4.

—SALMON & NANBAN SAUCE—

450 g (1 lb) salmon fillet, descaled
salt
plain flour for coating
vegetable oil for deep-frying
3 spring onions, shredded, to garnish
NANBAN SAUCE:
4 tablespoons shoyu
3 tablespoons rice vinegar
1½ tablespoons sake
2 teaspoons sugar
4½ tablespoons dashi, page 12
1-2 dried or fresh red chillies, deseeded and chopped

Cut the salmon fillet, with skin on, into 12 pieces and sprinkle with a pinch of salt.

Combine all the ingredients for the sauce in a saucepan and bring to the boil. Leave to cool. Pat dry the salmon pieces with absorbent kitchen paper and dredge in plain flour. Heat oil in a wok or a deep frying pan to 170C (340F). Shake off any excess flour from the salmon pieces and deep-fry for 3-4 minutes until golden brown. Drain on a wire rack.

Transfer the fried salmon pieces to a large serving plate and spread the shredded spring onion on top. Pour over the sauce and serve at once.

Serves 4.

──────SWORDFISH TERIYAKI──────

2-3 swordfish steaks, each weighing about 200-250 g
  (7-9 oz)
6 tablespoons shoyu
2 tablespoons sake
3 tablespoons mirin
4-5 fresh mint leaves, chopped
vegetable oil for frying
watercress sprigs, to garnish

Slice swordfish steaks in half horizontally to
make a thickness of 1 cm (½ in); cut into 6 x
4 cm (2½ x 1½ in) pieces. In a bowl, mix
shoyu, sake, mirin and mint, then add fish.
Mix well and leave to marinate for 30-40
minutes, turning over every now and then.

Heat a frying pan and spread a little oil
evenly over the base. Drain the fish pieces,
reserving the marinade and fry a few pieces
at a time over high heat until both sides
become dark brown.

When all the swordfish pieces are cooked
return them to the frying pan. Pour over the
marinade, gently fold it in and remove from
heat. Divide mixture between 4 individual
plates or heap it in the centre of a serving
plate. Garnish with sprigs of watercress and
serve at once.

Serves 4.

—SALT-SIMMERED SARDINES—

1 kg (2¼ lb) sardines, gutted
salt
lemon juice
5 cm (2 in) piece fresh root ginger, peeled and
    thinly sliced
2 dried red chillies
70 ml (2½ fl oz/⅓ cup) sake or white wine
lime slices, to garnish
LIME SAUCE:
1 lime juice
1 tablespoon shoyu
2 teaspoons mirin

Cut off sardine heads and rinse the bodies under cold running water.

Rinse in salted water (2 litres water to ½ cup salt). Drain and sprinkle with lemon juice. In a large frying pan or shallow saucepan, spread 2¼ teaspoons salt and half the ginger slices. Lay the sardines tightly on top. Put the rest of the ginger slices and another 2¼ teaspoons salt on the sardines and add the chillies. Place the pan over moderate heat and pour in the sake or wine. When it starts to warm up, add just enough water to cover the sardines. Place on top a piece of grease-proof paper cut to fit inside the pan.

Remove any residues floating on the surface and when the water is reduced to about one third remove the paper. Continue cooking until all the water evaporates (you will hear a sizzling noise) and remove from the heat. Mix all the ingredients for the lime sauce in a small bowl with 1 tablespoon water. Arrange 3-5 sardines each on individual plates, garnish with lime slices and serve with the lime sauce.

Serves 6-8.

-CHICKEN WITH WASABI SAUCE-

4 chicken breast fillets, trimmed
1 tablespoon sake
watercress sprigs and lemon slices, to garnish
WASABI SAUCE:
2 teaspoons wasabi paste or powder
3 tablespoons shoyu
juice of ½ lemon
1 tablespoon sake or white wine
5 g fresh chives, chopped

Separate each chicken fillet into two along its natural line.

Inserting the knife blade diagonally, slice the fillets crossways into pieces 1 cm (½ in) thick. Sprinkle with the sake. To make the wasabi sauce, mix wasabi paste, shoyu, lemon juice, sake or white wine and chopped chives. If using wasabi powder, mix with the same amount of water to make a paste, then mix with sauce ingredients.

Cook the chicken slices, a few slices at a time, in boiling water for 2 minutes (do not overcook), then plunge into ice cold water. Drain the slices and serve on individual plates, garnished with watercress and lemon slices and accompanied by small individual bowls of wasabi sauce.

Serves 4 as a starter.

–CHICKEN ROLLED ASPARAGUS–

4 chicken breast fillets
55 ml (2 fl oz/¼ cup) sake or white wine
salt and freshly ground black pepper
12 asparagus tips or 32-40 stalks french beans, trimmed
vegetable oil for frying
250 ml (8 fl oz/1 cup) dashi, page 12, or chicken stock
250 g (9 oz) spinach, trimmed
MUSTARD SAUCE:
2 teaspoons mustard
3 tablespoons shoyu

Cut chicken fillets in half along natural line and slice thickest half horizontally in two.

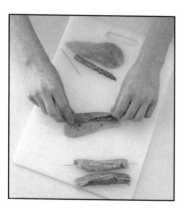

By making a few slits on thick parts even out the thickness to make 3 thin flat pieces, about 0.5 cm (¼ in) thick, per chicken breast. Sprinkle with a little of the sake and salt and pepper. Parboil the asparagus, or french beans, in lightly salted water and drain. Place a stalk of asparagus (or 4-5 french beans) on a chicken piece, roll up and secure with wooden cocktail sticks. If the asparagus is too long, trim to length of chicken. Repeat with rest of chicken and asparagus or beans. Heat oil in a frying pan and pan-fry chicken rolls until light golden.

Add rest of sake and dashi or stock, bring to boil, then simmer for 15 minutes. Cook spinach in boiling salted water for 1 minute, drain and chop into bite-size lengths. Dissolve mustard with shoyu and add 2-3 tablespoons of cooking juices to make a sauce. Cut the chicken rolls into bite-size pieces. Divide the spinach between 4 individual serving plates, heaping it into a nest, pour the sauce over the top, then arrange chicken pieces, cut-side up, on top.

Serves 4.

—CHICKEN & CABBAGE ROLLS—

450 g (1 lb) minced chicken
1 tablespoon each miso and shoyu
1 tablespoon sugar
salt
4 large leaves Savoy cabbage
4 spring onions, shredded
sake
cooked and shredded carrot, to garnish
MUSTARD SAUCE:
1-2 teaspoons mustard
2 tablespoons shoyu

Mix the minced chicken, miso, shoyu, sugar and a little salt and grind to a smooth paste, using the back of a tablespoon .

Trim the thick part of the central vein on the back of cabbage leaves, then parboil the leaves in lightly salted water. Place one leaf flat on a cutting board, trimmed side up and the bottom of the leaf nearest to you. Spread a quarter of the minced chicken paste evenly over top, leaving about 1 cm (½ in) margin from the top of the leaf. Arrange a quarter of the spring onion shreds crossways in the centre and roll up. Seal the edge with a wooden cocktail stick. Repeat to make 3 more rolls.

Place rolls on a large plate and sprinkle with sake. Place plate in a boiling steamer and steam the rolls over high heat for 15 minutes or until chicken meat is well cooked. Drain, remove the cocktail sticks and cut each roll diagonally into 4-5 pieces. Make a bed of shredded carrot on 4 individual serving plates and arrange the pieces of roll on top. In a jug, mix mustard and shoyu with 2-3 tablespoons of cooking juices. Pour sauce over chicken and cabbage and serve at once.

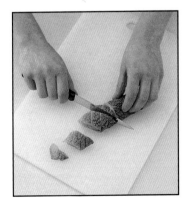

Serves 4 as a starter.

—GRILLED SKEWERED CHICKEN—

8 unskinned chicken thighs, boned
8 spring onions, white part only
24 okra, trimmed
lemon wedges, sansho peppers and chilli powder, to
  garnish
TARE SAUCE:
3 tablespoons sake
70 ml (2½ fl oz/⅓ cup) shoyu
1 tablespoon each mirin and sugar

Cut the chicken thighs into 2.5 cm (1 in) square pieces and spring onions crossways into 2.5 cm (1 in) lengths. Mix ingredients for the tare sauce in a saucepan and bring to the boil. Remove from heat and set aside.

If barbecuing, prepare the barbecue. Thread 4 pieces of chicken and 3 okra alternately onto a 20 cm (8 in) bamboo or stainless steel skewer. Repeat with another 7 skewers. Thread another 8 with 4 pieces of chicken and 3 pieces of spring onion. Thread any remaining ingredients onto extra skewers. Cook on the barbecue, keeping the skewer handles well away from the fire and turning them frequently. Brush with the tare sauce 2-3 times during cooking, until the chicken is well cooked and golden brown.

If grilling, preheat grill. On a well-oiled wire rack, spread chicken pieces well apart and cook under grill until both sides are golden brown. Dip pieces in tare sauce, put back on rack; grill for another 30 seconds on each side. Set aside. Lightly grill the spring onions and okra without dipping in sauce. Thread 4 chicken pieces alternately with 3 spring onions on 8 skewers and with okra on another 8. Serve on a platter, garnished with lemon, sansho peppers and chilli powder.

Serves 4-8 as a starter.

-CHAR-GRILLED YUAN CHICKEN-

4 whole chicken legs, boned
8 large spring onions, white part only
lime or lemon wedges, to garnish
MARINADE:
70 ml (2½ fl oz/⅓ cup) sake or white wine
70 ml (2½ oz/⅓ cup) mirin or 1 tablespoon
    sugar
70 ml (2½ fl oz/⅓ cup) shoyu
rind of 1 lemon or lime, in large pieces not chopped
    or shredded

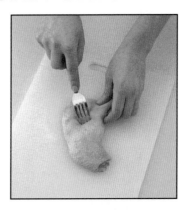

Place the chicken legs on a cutting board skin side up. Using a fork, pierce the skin in a few places. Cut the spring onions crossways into 4 cm (1½ in) lengths.

In a dish, mix all the marinade ingredients, add the chicken and spring onions and leave to marinate for 30 minutes. If barbecuing, prepare barbecue. Thread 3-4 long stainless steel skewers through each chicken leg parallel with the skin in a fan shape. Chargrill skin side down, over high heat for 6-7 minutes until golden brown, then turn and cook the other side for 3-4 minutes. Thread the spring onions, 6-8 pieces to a skewer, and char-grill. Remove skewers and serve 1 chicken leg and a quarter of the spring onion on each of 4 individual plates.

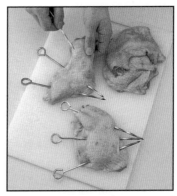

If grilling, preheat grill. Lay the chicken legs, unskewered, flat on a wire rack, with the skin side facing the heat first and grill for about 10 minutes until golden brown. Turn and grill the other side for 5-10 minutes until well cooked. Grill the spring onions until both sides are golden brown. Cut the chicken legs into bite-size pieces and arrange the chicken and spring onions on 4 individual plates. Serve hot, garnished with lime or lemon wedges.

Serves 4.

—FRIED FISH-STUFFED CHICKEN—

150-200g (5-7 oz) cod fillet, skinned
salt and freshly ground black pepper
4 chicken breast fillets, skinned
plain flour for coating
1 egg, beaten
dried breadcrumbs
vegetable oil for deep-frying
shredded lettuce, to garnish
DIPPING SAUCE:
6 tablespoons mayonnaise
1½ tablespoons shoyu

To make sauce, mix together mayonnaise
and shoyu. Set aside. Sprinkle the cod fillet
with a pinch of salt and pepper.

Separate one chicken fillet along its natural
divide into 2 pieces and cut the larger one
crossways into 4 pieces and the smaller one
into 2 pieces. Slice the 2 thickest pieces
horizontally in half to make 8 pieces of even
thickness, about 0.5 cm (¼ in). Repeat this
with the remaining 3 fillets. Make a deep slit
horizontally in the centre of each piece to
make chicken envelopes and stuff with small
pieces of the seasoned cod. The chicken
should completely encase the fish.

Dust stuffed chicken with plain flour, dip
into beaten egg, then roll in breadcrumbs
and press gently to seal chicken envelope
with the breadcrumbs. Heat the oil in a wok
or deep frying pan to 170C (340F) and deep-
fry the chicken pieces, a few at a time, for 5-
6 minutes until golden brown, turning frequently. Drain on a wire rack or absorbent
kitchen paper. Make a bed of shredded lettuce on 4 individual plates. Arrange chicken
on top. Serve at once with the sauce.

Serves 4.

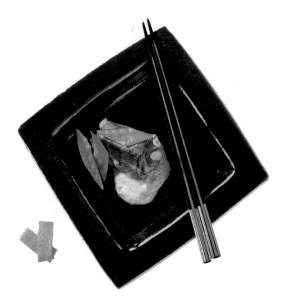

—COD ROE-STUFFED CHICKEN—

4 chicken thighs, boned and skinned
150 g (5 oz) smoked cod roe
vegetable oil and butter for frying
sake or white wine
parboiled mange tout (snow peas), to garnish
COD ROE MAYONNAISE:
4 tablespoons mayonnaise
1 tablespoon smoked cod roe, inside only
1 tablespoon mustard

Remove any fat from the chicken thighs and place on a cutting board, skinned side down. Open up the inner side by making several slits lengthways and even out the thickness.

Cut the cod roe lengthways into 5 strips and reserve one for making the sauce. Put a strip of cod roe on top of each chicken thigh, placing it lengthways in the centre. Roll in to the original thigh shape and seal the end with a wooden cocktail stick. Heat a frying pan, add a little vegetable oil and a knob of butter and fry the stuffed chicken thighs over high heat until both sides are golden brown. Drain on absorbent kitchen paper.

Transfer chicken to a large deep plate, or a shallow dish, and sprinkle generously with sake or white wine. Place the chicken in a boiling steamer and steam vigorously for 10-15 minutes until well cooked. Mix the mayonnaise, remaining cod roe and mustard and place a quarter in the centre of each of 4 individual plates. Remove chicken from steamer and drain. Remove cocktail sticks and place chicken on mayonnaise. Garnish with mange tout (snow peas) and serve.

Serves 4-6 as a starter.

–CHICKEN WITH ONION SAUCE–

8 chicken thighs, boned
sake, shoyu and sesame oil
1 egg, beaten
250 g (9 oz) broccoli, separated into flowerets
cornflour for coating
vegetable oil for deep-frying
red pepper (capsicum), shredded, to garnish
SPRING ONION SAUCE:
1-2 spring onions, finely chopped
2 tablespoons each shoyu and sake or white wine
2 tablespoons mirin or 2 teaspoons sugar
2 teaspoons sesame oil

Cut the chicken, with skin on, into bite-size pieces and put in a large mixing bowl.

Sprinkle generously with sake, shoyu and sesame oil and leave to marinate for about 15 minutes. Fold in the beaten egg and leave for another 15 minutes. Meanwhile, make the spring onion sauce by mixing all the ingredients in a bowl. Cook the broccoli in lightly salted boiling water for 3 minutes. Drain and keep warm. Roll the chicken pieces in cornflour and shake off the excess.

Heat vegetable oil in a wok or deep frying pan to 170C (340F) and fry chicken pieces, several at a time, until well cooked and light golden, turning frequently. (Do not add too much chicken at a time – the pan should not be more than two-thirds full at any time.) Drain well on a wire rack or absorbent kitchen paper and arrange in the centre of a serving platter along with the broccoli. Pour the sauce over the top, sprinkle with the red pepper (capsicum) and serve at once.

Serves 4.

GINGER PORK

450 g (1 lb) pork fillets or boneless chops
5 cm (2 in) piece fresh root ginger, peeled and
  grated
4 tablespoons shoyu
boiled rice and lightly cooked mange tout (snow
  peas), to garnish

Inserting the blade of a knife diagonally, slice the pork fillets crossways into very thin, 2.5 cm (1 in) diameter discs. If using chops, discard fat and cut roughly into 5 x 2.5 cm (2 x 1 in) thin pieces.

Place pork slices on a large plate, spreading as widely apart as possible, and sprinkle all over with the grated ginger, together with its juice, and the shoyu. Leave to marinate for 15 minutes.

Heat a frying pan, add 2-3 tablespoons vegetable oil and fry the pork slices for 2-3 minutes on each side until they are well cooked and both sides are golden brown. Arrange a quarter of the cooked pork slices on a bed of boiled rice, garnish with the mange tout (snow peas) and serve at once.

Serves 4.

FRIED PORK CUTLETS

4 pork loin cutlets or boneless chops
salt and freshly ground black pepper
plain flour for coating
2 eggs, beaten
dried breadcrumbs for coating
vegetable oil for deep-frying
shredded cabbage and lemon wedges, to garnish
TONKATSU SAUCE:
4 tablespoons tomato ketchup (sauce)
1 tablespoon shoyu
2 teaspoons Worcestershire sauce
2 teaspoons mustard plus extra for serving

Make a few slits in the fat of the cutlets or chops to prevent them curling when cooked.

Sprinkle both sides of the pork cutlets with salt and pepper and dredge with flour, shaking off any excess. Dip in the beaten egg, then coat in breadcrumbs. Heat oil in a wok or a deep frying pan to 180C (350F). Gently slide in the pork cutlets, 1 or 2 at a time, and deep-fry for 5-7 minutes until golden brown, turning once or twice. Drain on absorbent kitchen paper. In between each batch, clean the oil with a mesh ladle. Meanwhile, mix all the ingredients for the sauce in a small serving bowl.

When all the cutlets have been cooked, place them on a cutting board and cut each one crossways into 2.5 cm (1 in) lengths. Arrange the cutlets on 4 individual plates and garnish with very finely shredded raw cabbage and lemon wedges. Serve with the sauce and extra mustard, if wished.

Serves 4.

Note: This dish is called Tonkatsu in Japanese.

—PORK WITH CITRUS SHOYU—

450 g (1 lb) pork loin or gammon
3 spring onions, cut in half
5 cm (2 in) piece fresh root ginger, peeled and cut
    into 3-4 pieces
salt
CITRUS SHOYU:
juice of ½ lemon
1 tablespoon each lime juice and rice vinegar
2 tablespoons shoyu and ½ tablespoon mirin
2 spring onions, finely chopped
2.5 cm (1 in) piece fresh root ginger, peeled and
    finely chopped

In a large pot, put pork, onions, ginger and
and a pinch of salt and cover with water.

Bring to boil, cover pot and simmer gently
for 2 hours. Drain the meat, put it in a bowl
of ice cold water and refrigerate until
chilled. Remove the pork from the water,
pat dry and then slice it crossways against
the grain as thinly as possible. Arrange the
slices, fanning them out around the edge of
a large serving platter.

To make the citrus shoyu, mix all the
ingredients together and stir well until the
sugar has dissolved. Transfer it to a serving
bowl or a ramekin and place in the centre of
the pork circle. Serve cold.

Serves 4.

─GRILLED PORK WITH MISO─

4 pork loin steaks
lemon wedges, to garnish
MISO SAUCE:
3 tablespoons red miso
3 spring onions, finely chopped
2 teaspoons sake
2 teaspoons fresh root ginger juice

Remove any fat from the pork. If the pork is more than 1.5 cm (⅔ in) thick, slice in half horizontally.

Preheat grill. Heat a well-oiled wire rack under the hot grill and place the pork steaks on it. Gently grill the pork for 3-4 minutes on each side or until both sides are golden brown and well cooked.

In a mixing bowl, make the miso sauce by mixing all the ingredients. Lower the heat and remove the rack from the grill. Spoon the miso sauce evenly onto the centre of the pork steaks and put back under medium hot grill for 1 minute until the miso sauce is fairly dry. Transfer the steaks to 4 individual plates, garnish with lemon wedges and serve.

Serves 4.

—STEAK WITH GRATED DAIKON—

4 fillet or sirloin steaks, about 250 g (9 oz) each
vegetable oil
2 tablespoons butter
brandy for sprinkling
½ small onion, grated
shoyu
1 spring onion, finely chopped
cress and lemon slices, to garnish
DAIKON RELISH:
10 cm (4 in) piece of large daikon, peeled and grated
2 teaspoons wasabi paste

To make relish, lightly squeeze out the water from grated daikon, reserving the water. Put daikon in a bowl and mix in wasabi paste.

With the tip of a blade, cut the veins of the steaks to prevent them from shrinking when cooked. Heat a little oil and ½ tablespoon of butter per steak and fry the steaks, 1 or 2 at a time, to your liking. Sprinkle with a little brandy. When the alcohol burns out, remove steaks from the pan, cut crossways into 5 cm (2 in) strips and keep warm.

Skim off oil from pan, add grated onion and quickly stir-fry. Pour the reserved water from the grated daikon into the pan and add 2-3 tablespoons shoyu. When mixture is warm, put 2-3 tablespoons on each of 4 individual plates and place a sliced steak on top. Arrange the daikon relish on the steak and sprinkle with the chopped spring onion. Garnish with cress and lemon slices and serve hot.

Serves 4.

—BEEF SALAD WITH AUBERGINE—

450 g (1 lb) rump steak
salt and freshly ground pepper
1 large aubergine (eggplant), trimmed
vegetable oil for deep-frying
150 g (5 oz) okra, trimmed
GINGER SHOYU:
2 tablespoons fresh root ginger juice
55 ml (2 fl oz/¼ cup) shoyu
3 tablespoons wine vinegar
1 tablespoon sake

Sprinkle the steak with salt and pepper. Cut aubergine (eggplant) into bite-size pieces. Prepare the ginger shoyu by mixing all the ingredients together, then set aside.

Heat vegetable oil in a wok or a deep frying pan to about 170C (340F) and quickly deep fry aubergine (eggplant) pieces and whole okra for about 1 minute. Drain on absorbent kitchen paper.

Heat a frying pan and add a little vegetable oil. Add steak and fry on high heat until both sides are golden brown and cooked to your liking. Turn out on to a slightly damp cutting board, leave to cool and cut in half lengthways and then crossways into 0.5 cm (¼ in) thick slices. Put the steak, aubergine (eggplant) and okra in a large serving bowl, pour over the ginger shoyu and toss well. Serve warm or chilled.

Serves 4-6.

——————BEEF TERIYAKI——————

150-200 g (5-7 oz) asparagus tips
salt
100 ml (3½ fl oz/½ cup) dashi, page 12
4 tablespoons shoyu
4 sirloin or rump steaks, about 250 g (9 oz) each
vegetable oil
4 tablespoons sake or white wine
3 tablespoons mirin or 1 tablespoon sugar
mustard, to serve

Boil asparagus tips in lightly salted water for 3 minutes, drain, cool under cold running water and pat dry. In a bowl, mix the dashi and 2 tablespoons of the shoyu, pour it over asparagus and leave to marinate.

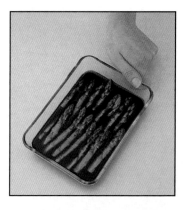

Lightly salt the steaks and fry in a little oil over high heat, covered, for 3 minutes on one side. Turn over and while second side is frying sprinkle the meat with 1 tablespoon sake or white wine per steak. Cover the pan and fry for another 2-3 minutes. Remove the steaks to a plate.

Add the remaining shoyu and the mirin or sugar to the pan and mix with the meat cooking juices. Return the steaks to the pan and coat them on both sides with the teriyaki sauce. Turn out on to a cutting board and cut the steaks crossways into 1.5 cm (⅔ in) slices. Arrange the steaks on individual plates and spoon over some teriyaki sauce. Garnish with the asparagus tips and serve with mustard.

Serves 4.

BEEF TATAKI

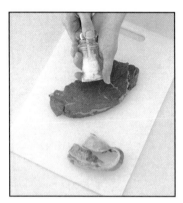

450 g (1 lb) lean sirloin steak
salt and vegetable oil for brushing
2 spring onions, finely chopped
2.5 cm (1 in) piece fresh root ginger, peeled and
    grated
1 tablespoon wasabi paste
½ cucumber
lime slices and watercress, to garnish
DAIKON DIP:
7.5 cm (3 in) daikon (mooli), peeled and grated
3 tablespoons shoyu
juice of ½ lime

Preheat grill. Trim fat from meat, sprinkle
with a pinch of salt and brush with oil.

Quickly brown under a high grill for 2-3
minutes on each side. Remove from the heat
and immediately plunge into ice cold water
to stop further cooking. Traditionally the
meat should be golden brown outside but
rare inside. Drain, pat dry and set aside while
preparing the daikon dip. Mix the grated
daikon, shoyu and lime juice in a serving
bowl. Arrange the chopped spring onions,
grated ginger and wasabi in separate heaps
on a small plate. Cut the cucumber in half
lengthways, then slice crossways into paper-
thin 'half-moons'.

Slice the meat very thinly against the grain.
Arange each piece folded on a half-moon
slice of cucumber, slightly overlapping in a
circle on a large serving platter. Garnish
with lime slices and watercress. Serve with
the bowl of daikon dip, accompanied by the
plate of condiments. Each diner has a small
plate for mixing their own dip sauce.

Serves 4-6.

Note: Serve this dish with 'autumn maple
leaf' relish, see page 28, if liked.

— SIMMERED BEEF & POTATOES —

300 g (10 oz) piece of lean beef
5 medium potatoes, peeled
2 Spanish onions
2 tablespoons vegetable oil
5 tablespoons sugar
6 tablespoons shoyu
dashi, page 12, or water
parboiled mange tout (snow peas), to garnish

Put the beef in the freezer for about 1 hour to part-harden, then slice very thinly against the grain into bite-size pieces.

Quarter each potato and boil until tender but still slightly hard in the centre. Drain and set aside. Cut the onions into thin half-moon slices. In a frying pan or a shallow saucepan, heat a little vegetable oil and stir-fry the beef slices over medium heat. When the beef begins to change colour, add the potatoes and continue to stir. Add the sugar and shoyu to the pan and lightly fold in. Pour in enough dashi or water to just cover the ingredients and bring to the boil. Skim the surface and lower the heat.

Place a small wooden lid or a plate touching the ingredients inside the pan and simmer over medium heat for 10 minutes. Add the onion slices and continue to cook until all ingredients are tender and have absorbed the flavour. Serve in small individual bowls garnished with mange tout (snow peas).

Serves 4.

─── MIXED GRIDDLE ───

300 g (10 oz) sirloin or topside of beef or 2 chicken
    breast fillets, skinned
1 squid, cleaned (optional)
4-8 scallops or raw jumbo (king) prawns, peeled
4-8 fresh shiitake or button mushrooms, stalks
    removed
1 red or green pepper (capsicum), deseeded
250 g (9 oz) bean sprouts, trimmed
1 lemon, cut into wedges
2-3 spring onions, finely chopped
vegetable oil for frying
DIPPING SAUCE:
15 cm (6 in) large daikon (mooli), peeled
1 fresh or dried chilli
shoyu

Prepare wafer-thin beef slices following the
method used for Sukiyaki, opposite. Skin
the squid by holding the two flaps together
and peeling down; cut in half lengthways.
Put fillets on a cutting board skinned-side up
and make fine cross slits on them with a
sharp knife. Cut fillets and flaps into 2.5 cm
(1 in) square pieces. Separate the tentacles,
if large. Arrange the meat and the fish on
separate platters. If the mushrooms are large,
cut them in half. Slice pepper (capsicum)
into thin strips. Arrange all the vegetables
on a platter.

Make 'autumn maple leaf' relish following
the method on page 28, or, alternatively,
grate the daikon, finely chop the fresh chilli
and simply mix together. Arrange daikon
relish, lemon wedges and the spring onion in
a serving bowl or on small plate. Place a hotplate in the centre of the dining table set
with small individual bowls. Serve the meat,
fish and vegetable platters and condiments:
diners mix their own sauce, adding shoyu to
taste, and fry their portion for themselves.

Serves 4-6.

—SUKIYAKI (PAN-COOKED BEEF)—

450 g (1 lb) sirloin or topside of beef
2 leeks, white part only
8 fresh or dried shiitake or button mushrooms,
  stalks removed if fresh
sugar
250 g (9 oz) (1 cake) tofu
115 g (4 oz) watercress, trimmed
5 cm (2 in) square of beef fat
70 ml (2½ oz/⅓ cup) sake or white wine
55 ml (2 fl oz/¼ cup) shoyu

Trim off any fat from the beef and cut the beef into 7.5 x 4 cm (3 x 1½ in) flat pieces (any length).

Place in separate freezer bags and freeze for 1-2 hours. Take out of freezer and leave until half-thawed. Cut the beef into wafer-thin slices and arrange in a circular fan on a large platter. Slice the leeks diagonally. If the shiitake mushrooms are large, cut in half. If using dried shiitake, soak in warm water with a pinch of sugar for 45 minutes, then remove stalks. Cut the tofu into 16 cubes. Arrange all the vegetables and tofu on a large platter.

Place a cast-iron frying pan on a portable gas ring or electric hotplate on the table together with the platters of raw ingredients, jugs of water, the shoyu and sake and a sugar pot. Melt the beef fat in the pan and move around to oil the entire base. Cook a few slices of beef first, then add some of the other ingredients and sprinkle with about 2 tablespoons sugar. Pour in the sake and shoyu, and add water to taste. Diners serve themselves into individual small bowls.

Serves 4.

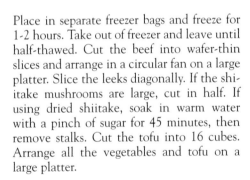

–SHABUSHABU (BEEF HOT POT)–

450 g (1 lb) sirloin or topside of beef
2 leeks, white part only
8 fresh or dried shiitake or 12 button mushrooms,
   stalks removed
250 g (9 oz) (1 cake) firm tofu
4-6 Chinese cabbage (hakusai) leaves
300 g (10 oz) spinach, trimmed
10 cm (4 in) piece dried konbu (kelp)
300 g (10 oz) udon noodles, cooked (optional)
finely chopped spring onion, to garnish
CITRUS DIP:
½ daikon (mooli), peeled
1 dried or fresh red chilli
2 spring onions, finely chopped
juice of ½ lemon and ½ lime
115 ml (4 fl oz/½ cup) shoyu

SESAME DIP:
4 tablespoons sesame paste or smooth peanut butter
115 ml (4 fl oz/½ cup) dashi, page 12
3 tablespoons shoyu
1 tablespoons mirin or sweet sherry
1 tablespoon sugar
2 tablespoons sake or white wine
2 teaspoons chilli oil or chilli powder (optional)

Trim off any fat from the beef and cut into
7.5 x 4 cm (3 x 1½ in) flat pieces (any
length). Place in separate freezer bags and
freeze for 1-2 hours.

Remove from the freezer and leave until half
thawed, then cut the beef into wafer-thin
slices and arrange in a circular fan on a large
platter. Slice leeks diagonally. If the shiitake
mushrooms are large cut in half. If using
dried shiitake, soak in warm water with a
pinch of sugar for 45 minutes, then remove
stalks before use. Cut the tofu into 16 cubes.
Cut the Chinese cabbage leaves and spinach
into bite-size pieces. Arrange the vegetables
and tofu on a large platter.

To prepare the citrus dip, first make 'autumn maple leaf' relish, following the method on page 28. Alternatively, grate the daikon very finely and chop the fresh red chilli, then mix together. Put the relish, chopped spring onion, a mixture of the lemon and lime juices, and the shoyu in separate small bowls. To make the sesame dip, mix all the ingredients together and stir until the sesame paste (or peanut butter) is of a smooth runny consistency. Divide between 4-6 individual dipping bowls.

Put the konbu in a large pot (ideally a clay pot, an enamelled cast-iron casserole or a copper-based Mongolian hot-pot) and fill two thirds full with water. Bring to the boil and remove the konbu. Put in some of the leek, Chinese leaves, shiitake mushrooms, spinach and tofu and when it begins to come back to boil, transfer the pot to a portable gas ring or electric hotplate on the dining table. Diners make their own citrus dip in individual dipping bowls by mixing 1-2 teaspoons each of the relish, spring onion and citrus juice with some shoyu.

Diners serve themselves by cooking the meat in the pot, adding more vegetables, and eating them dipped in either of the sauces. When ingredients are finished, skim and season the soup with shoyu and a little salt and sugar. If using noodles, warm them in the soup, seasoned with a little shoyu to taste, so that diners can end the meal with plain noodles garnished with chopped spring onion.

Serves 4-6.

——TOFU & FISH HOT POT——

500 g (1 lb 2oz) (2 cakes) tofu
250 g (9 oz) white fish steak or fillets, such as cod
4 Chinese cabbage (hakusai) leaves
55 g (2 oz) coriander leaves and/or 200 g (7 oz)
    spinach, trimmed
2-3 spring onions, finely chopped
SOUP:
15 cm (6 in) piece dried konbu (kelp) (optional)
500 ml (18 fl oz/2½ cups) dashi, page 12
3 tablespoons shoyu
½ tablespoon sugar

Cut the tofu into bite-size cubes and the fish steaks or fillets into chunks with the bone and skin still on.

Cut the Chinese leaves in half lengthways and then crossways into 2.5 cm (1 in) long pieces. Chop the coriander leaves and/or spinach roughly into 5 cm (2 in) lengths.

To make the soup, put the konbu in a pot (ideally a clay pot or enamelled casserole) and add the dashi, shoyu and sugar. Bring to the boil and then add some of each of the prepared ingredients. When it begins to boil again, transfer pot to a portable gas ring or electric hotplate on the dining table. Diners then serve themselves to some soup and ingredients in individual bowls, sprinkled with chopped spring onion.

Serves 4.

ISHIKARI HOT POT

4 salmon steaks, scaled
1 onion
2 potatoes and 1-2 carrots
4-8 fresh shiitake or button mushrooms
55 g (2 oz) coriander leaves or watercress
250 g (9 oz) (1 cake) firm tofu
300 g (10 oz) (1 cake) konnyaku (optional)
25 g (1 oz) butter
10 cm (4 in) piece dried konbu (kelp) (optional)
3-5 tablespoons miso
2 spring onions, finely chopped

Leaving the skin on, cut the salmon steaks into chunky pieces. Cut onion in half and slice into 0.5 cm (¼ in) thick half-moons.

Slice potatoes and carrots into 1 cm (½ in) thick discs (if large, cut into half-moons) and parboil separately. Drain and set aside. Slice the shiitake mushrooms diagonally into 4 slices. Chop coriander leaves or watercress into 6 cm (2½ in) lengths. Cut the tofu and konnyaku, if using, in half lengthways, then cut the tofu into 1 cm (½ in) squares and the konnyaku into 0.5 cm (¼ in) slices. Melt butter in a large cast-iron pot and stir-fry onion slices for 1-2 minutes. Add konbu and enough water to half fill pot.

Bring to the boil over medium heat, discard konbu and lower heat. Dissolve the miso in a bowl with some of soup, then stir back into pan. Add potatoes, carrots, salmon, shiitake and konnyaku, then cover and cook over low heat for 5 minutes. Add coriander or watercress and tofu; simmer for 3-4 minutes. Serve sprinkled with chopped spring onion.

Serves 4-6.

Note: Ishikari is a river on the northern island of Japan which is famous for salmon.

—SUMO WRESTLERS' HOT POT—

1.5 kg (3¼-3½ lb) whole chicken
10 cm (4 in) piece dried konbu (kelp) (optional)
250-300 g (9-10 oz) whole fish, such as trout
6 Chinese cabbage (hakusai) leaves
2 carrots
12-18 raw king (jumbo) prawns, peeled
12-18 shiitake or button mushrooms, stalks
   removed
250 g (9 oz) broccoli, separated into flowerets
12 mochi rice cakes (optional)
CITRUS DIP:
½ daikon (mooli), peeled
2 dried or fresh red chillies
2 spring onions, finely chopped
juice of 1 lemon and ½ lime
6 tablespoons shoyu

Cut the chicken, including skin and bones, into 4-5 cm (1½-2 in) square pieces, clean and wash in boiling water. Drain and put in a large pot. Add the konbu, if using, and half fill the pot with water. Bring to the boil over high heat, remove the konbu and simmer the chicken for 30 minutes, occasionally skimming off any scum from the surface of the liquid. Meanwhile, scale the fish and cut roughly into 5 cm (2 in) long chunky pieces. Cut the Chinese cabbage into bite-size pieces and the carrots into thin rounds. Arrange all the ingredients on a platter.

To prepare citrus dip, make 'autumn maple leaf' relish, following the method on page 28, and put in a serving bowl with the chopped spring onion. In a jug, mix the lemon and lime juices and shoyu. Transfer the chicken hot-pot to a portable gas ring or electric hotplate on the dining table set with individual dipping bowls and the citrus dip ingredients. Diners make their own dip and serve themselves.

Serves 6-8.

ODEN

300 g (10 oz) (1 cake) konnyaku
½ daikon (mooli), peeled
1-2 turnips
2-3 potatoes
12 fish balls or cakes
4 eggs, hard-boiled and shelled
mustard for serving
SOUP:
500 ml (18 oz/2½ cups) chicken stock
500 ml (18 oz/2½ cups) dashi, page 12
115 ml (4 fl oz/½ cup) shoyu
115 ml (4 fl oz/½ cup) mirin or sake and
   2 tablespoons sugar
1 teaspoon salt

Cut konnyaku cake in half, then diagonally
quarter each half to make 8 triangles. Cut
daikon and turnips in half lengthways, then
into 2.5 cm (1 in) thick half-moon slices.
Cook both lots of slices in boiling water
until tender and drain. Cut potatoes in half,
or quarter them if large, and parboil. To
make soup, in a large earthenware pot or a
flameproof casserole, heat the chicken stock
and dashi over low heat, then add shoyu and
mirin or sake and salt.

Add konnyaku triangles, vegetables, fish
balls and eggs and simmer, uncovered, for
1 hour. Bring the cooking pot to the dining
table for diners to help themselves. Serve
with mustard.

Serves 4.

Note: There are many types of ready-to-
cook oden ingredients, such as fish balls and
cakes, in packets at Japanese supermarkets.

RICE BALLS

400 g (14 oz/2 cups) Japanese rice
salt
160 g (5½ oz) salmon steak
55 g (2 oz) smoked cod roe, skinned
2 teaspoons sake
red chilli powder (optional)
2 tablespoons black or white sesame seeds
1-2 sheets of nori (wafer-thin dried seaweed),
    optional
Chinese Leaves & Kimchee, page 32, to garnish

Boil rice following the method on page 17. Heavily salt the salmon and leave for at least 30 minutes. Preheat grill.

Wipe off the salt from the salmon with absorbent kitchen paper and grill salmon under high heat until both sides are lightly burnt. Remove the skin and break flesh into rough flakes. Put cod roe in a small bowl, sprinkle with the sake and make into a paste. Add a pinch of chilli powder, if wished. Put the sesame seeds in a small saucepan and quickly toss over high heat. Place a sheet of nori over low heat and swiftly turn over a few times to bring out the flavour. Using kitchen scissors, cut it into 8 pieces. Repeat if using a second sheet.

Put 2 tablespoons rice into each of 4 wet teacups. Make a hole in centre of each, put 1 teaspoonful salmon into each one and press to cover with rice. Wet hands and rub with salt. Turn out rice onto your hand and squeeze, shaping it into a round. Sprinkle with sesame seeds and partly wrap with nori. Make 4 more with cod roe inside but with no sesame seeds. Mix rest of the rice with remaining ingredients to make 4 or 5 rice balls. Garnish with salted leaves and serve.

Makes about 12.

CHESTNUT RICE

400 g (14 oz/2 cups) Japanese rice
1½ teaspoons salt
2 tablespoons sake
150 g (5 oz) fresh chestnuts, shelled and peeled
    or 250 g (9 oz) cooked peeled chestnuts
lightly toasted black sesame seeds, to garnish

Put the rice in a deep enamelled cast-iron casserole and wash well, changing the water several times until the water becomes clear. Leave to soak in just enough water to cover the rice for 1 hour. If using fresh chestnuts, cut them in half and gently rinse in cold water. Drain and place on top of rice.

In a measuring jug, dissolve salt with 250 ml (9 fl oz/1 cup) water and add to pan. Add extra water, if necessary, to make water level 2.5 cm (1 in) above the rice and chestnuts. Pour in the sake, cover and cook over high heat for 8-10 minutes until mixture begins to sizzle. Lower heat and simmer for a further 10 minutes until water is absorbed. Leave to stand, still covered, for 10-15 minutes, then gently mix chestnuts into rice. Serve in rice bowls sprinkled with sesame seeds.

If using cooked chestnuts, cut large ones in half. In a measuring jug, dissolve salt with 250 ml (9 fl oz/1 cup) water and add to rice. Add extra water, if necessary, to make the level 1.5 cm (⅔ in) above rice. Pour in the sake, cover and cook over high heat for 7-8 minutes until mixture sizzles. Lower heat, add chestnuts and simmer, covered, for 10 minutes until water is absorbed. Let stand, covered, for 10-15 minutes. Gently mix the chestnuts into rice and serve as above.

Serves 4-6.

BABY CLAM RICE

600 g (1⅓ lb/3 cups) Japanese rice
2 tablespoons sake or white wine
2 tablespoons shoyu
1 teaspoon sugar
250 g (9 oz) canned baby clams, drained
⅔ teaspoon salt
2 spring onions, finely shredded

Put the rice in a deep enamelled cast-iron casserole and wash well, changing the water several times until the water becomes clear. Leave to soak in just enough water to cover the rice for 1 hour.

Meanwhile, in a saucepan mix sake, shoyu and sugar over high heat and quickly toss in the clams. Skim surface and remove from heat. Pour juice from pan into a measuring jug and keep the clams warm in the pan.

Drain rice. Add enough water to jug to make pan juices up to 250 ml (9 fl oz/ 1 cup) and dissolve the salt in it. Pour mixture over the rice, cover and place on high heat. Bring to boil and cook for 7-8 minutes until it sizzles, then lower heat and simmer for 10 minutes. Place clams and spring onions on top. Cover and cook over high heat for 2 seconds. Remove from heat and leave to stand for 10-15 minutes. Gently mix clams and spring onions into the rice. Serve in rice bowls.

Serves 4-6.

TEMPURA RICE BOWL

600 g (1⅓ lb/3 cups) Japanese rice
12 raw king (jumbo) prawns
12 okra, trimmed
1 egg
115 g (4 oz/1 cup) plain flour
vegetable oil for deep-frying
TARE SAUCE:
2 tablespoons sugar
3 tablespoons shoyu
115 ml (4 fl oz/½ cup) dashi, page 12

Boil rice following method on page 17 and
keep warm. Peel prawns, retaining tail shell,
and remove black vein. Make a slit along
the belly to prevent curling during cooking.

To make tare sauce, dissolve sugar with the
dashi and shoyu in a saucepan over medium
heat and set aside. Beat egg in a measuring
jug and add enough water to make up to
250 ml (9 fl oz/1 cup). Add the flour to the
jug and gently fold in a few times: do not stir
as the batter should be lumpy. Heat oil in a
wok or deep frying pan to 170C (340F).
Plunge the prawns and okra, one or two at a
time, into the batter and deep-fry until light
golden. Drain on absorbent kitchen paper.

Divide the rice between 4 large individual
bowls. Pour about 1 tablespoon of the tare
sauce over each portion. Arrange 3 prawns
and 3 okra on top of each portion of rice and
pour the remaining tare sauce over the top.
Serve hot.

Serves 4.

Note: Cold left-over tempura, see page 46,
can be used for this dish. Gently reheat the
tempura in the tare sauce before placing it
on top of boiled rice.

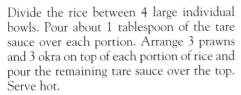

—CHICKEN & EGG RICE BOWL—

600 g (1⅓ lb/3 cups) Japanese rice
2 chicken breast fillets
vegetable oil for frying
2 onions, halved and sliced
4 eggs
cress, to garnish
COOKING SAUCE:
salt and 250 ml (9 fl oz/1 cup) dashi, page 12
1 tablespoon sake or white wine
2 tablespoons each shoyu and sugar

Boil the rice following method on page 17 and keep warm. Cut chicken fillets in half along natural dividing line and thinly slice crossways, inserting knife blade diagonally.

In a saucepan, heat all the sauce ingredients over medium heat until sugar has dissolved. Remove from the heat and set aside. Place a small (pancake-size) frying pan over high heat and spread a little oil over the base, then fry ¼ of the chicken slices for about 2 minutes or until both sides are a light golden brown. Add ¼ of the onion slices and stir-fry for 1 minute.

Pour ¼ of the cooking sauce into the pan and when hot pour a beaten egg over it. Cover and cook until egg hardens. Divide the boiled rice between 4 large individual bowls. With a spatula, turn out chicken and egg mixture into a bowl of boiled rice and pour over the sauce. Repeat this 3 more times to make 4 individual chicken and egg rice bowls. Serve hot, garnished with cress.

Serves 4.

TONKATSU RICE BOWL

600 g (1⅓ lb/3 cups) Japanese rice
4 pork loin steaks
plain flour
2 eggs, beaten
dried breadcrumbs
vegetable oil for deep-frying
1 leek, sliced diagonally
4 whole eggs
watercress, to garnish
COOKING SAUCE:
2 teaspoons mustard
115 ml (4 fl oz/½ cup) dashi, page 12, or water
4 tablespoons shoyu
2 tablespoons tomato ketchup (sauce) or fruit sauce

Boil the rice following the method on page 17 and keep warm. Make 4 fried pork cutlets (tonkatsu), page 62. Cut the fried cutlets crossways into 1.5 cm (⅔ in) wide pieces. In a measuring jug, mix mustard with the dashi, shoyu and tomato ketchup (sauce) or fruit sauce. Place a small frying pan over high heat, add a quarter of the sauce and bring to the boil over high heat. Add a quarter of the leek and cook for 1-2 minutes. Place a sliced cutlet on top and spoon over the sauce from the side.

Pour a beaten egg on top of the cutlet. Cover and simmer over low heat until egg hardens. Put a quarter of the rice in an individual noodle bowl. Using a spatula, place cutlet and leek slices on top and pour sauce over the top. Repeat 3 more times with remaining ingredients to make 4 rice bowls. Serve garnished with watercress.

Serves 4.

Note: This is an ideal recipe for using up cold left-over fried pork cutlets.

STEAK RICE BOWL

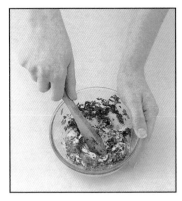

600 g (1⅓ lb/3 cups) Japanese rice
55 g (2 oz) butter
2 tablespoons chopped fresh parsley
2 tablespoons lemon juice
4 fillet or sirloin steaks, about 250 g (9 oz) each
salt and freshly ground black pepper
butter and vegetable oil for frying
brandy
1 onion, cut into rings
watercress, to garnish

Boil the rice following method on page 17 and keep warm. Meanwhile, in a small bowl, cream the 55 g (2 oz) butter, then mix in the chopped parsley and the lemon juice.

Sprinkle the steaks with a pinch of salt and pepper. Place a frying pan over high heat and melt a knob of butter in a little oil. Fry the steaks, one at a time, until both sides are golden brown, sprinkle with a little brandy and cook for a few seconds until cooked to your liking. Turn out onto a cutting board and cut into 1 cm (½ in) slices.

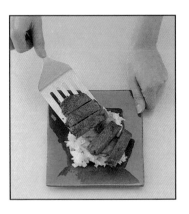

Divide the boiled rice between 4 individual noodle bowls. Heat a little vegetable oil in a small frying pan and stir-fry the onion over high heat until golden brown. Season with salt and pepper. Divide the onion between the bowls of rice and place a steak on top of each one. Dot each steak with a quarter of the creamed butter mixture and serve hot, garnished with watercress.

Serves 4.

──── TRICOLOUR LUNCH BOX ────

300 g (10 oz/2 cups) Japanese rice
13 teaspoons sugar
3 tablespoons shoyu
salt and 4 tablespoons sake
250 g (9 oz) minced chicken
3 eggs, beaten
cooked mange tout (snow peas), to garnish

Wash rice, cover with water and soak for 30 minutes. In a measuring jug, mix 1 teaspoon sugar, 1 tablespoon shoyu, ½ teaspoon salt and 1 tablespoon sake. Add enough water to make up to 250 ml (9 fl oz/ 1 cup), then pour the mixture onto the rice.

Adjust water level to come 1.5 cm (⅔ in) above the rice and cook, covered, over high heat for 6-7 minutes until it sizzles. Lower the heat and simmer for 10 minutes, without taking the lid off. Keep warm. Put minced chicken in a saucepan with 3 tablespoons sake, 2 tablespoons shoyu and 1 tablespoon sugar and cook over medium heat. stirring, until all the juice evaporates and the meat turns to granules. In a separate saucepan, cook the beaten eggs with the remaining sugar and salt, stirring constantly, until finely granulated, then set aside.

Divide the boiled rice between 4 individual lunch boxes. Put a quarter of the chicken on one half of the surface of the rice and one quarter of the granulated egg on the other half. Garnish with mange tout (snow peas).

Makes 4 lunch boxes.

Note: In addition to mange tout (snow peas), garnish the lunch boxes with a 'cherry blossom' vinegared radish, see page 33, in the centre, if wished.

—HOMEMADE UDON—

750 g (1⅔ lbs./3½ cups) white plain flour
1½ tablespoons salt

Put the flour in a large mixing bowl and make a well in the centre. Dissolve the salt in 250 ml (9 fl oz./1 cup) water, pour into the well in the flour and gently fold in to make a firm dough. The dough should be fairly dry but if it is still crumbly add a little more water. Turn onto a pastry board and knead vigorously until smooth but still firm. Hit it hard with a fist at least 100 times to remove any air pockets and make it an oval shape.

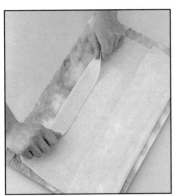

Cover dough with a clean damp tea towel and leave for at least 2 hours. Turn out onto a lightly floured pastry board and roll out, dusting with flour if necessary, to make a very thin, not more than 0.3 cm (⅛ in) thick, rectangular sheet. Dust the surface of the pastry with flour, then fold from both sides into the centre, turn over, dust with flour and fold in half.

Using a sharp knife, cut the folded pastry crossways into 0.3 cm (⅛ in) thick strips. Separate the strands with your hands. Cook in a very large deep saucepan with plenty of boiling water for 25-30 minutes, adding some cold water each time it starts boiling, until noodles are cooked to the core but still retain some crunchiness. Drain and wash well under running water to remove the outer starch from the noodles. This makes about 900 g (2 lb) of noodles.

Serves 4.

————————POT-COOKED UDON————————

4 fresh or dried shiitake or any mushrooms,
  stalks removed, plus sugar and shoyu if using
  dried shiitake
900 g (2 lb) fresh cooked udon noodles or
  400 g (14 oz) dried uncooked udon noodles
4 raw king (jumbo) prawns
4 fish balls or cakes (optional)
55 g (2 oz) cress or watercress
4 eggs
BROTH:
1.35 litres (48 fl oz/6 cups) second dashi, page 12,
  or water and 2 teaspoons dashi-no-moto (freeze-
  dried dashi powder)
1½ teaspoons salt
4 tablespoons shoyu
1 tablespoon sugar and 2 tablespoons mirin

Make a cross slit on top of fresh shiitake
caps. If using dried ones, soak in warm water
with a pinch of sugar for about 1 hour, then
cook in mixture of 115 ml (4 fl oz/½ cup) of
the soaking water and 2 tablespoons each of
sugar and shoyu. Meanwhile, if using dried
udon noodles cook them in plenty of boiling
water until tender, following the packet
instructions. Wash away the starch from the
noodles under running water and drain. Mix
all the ingredients for the broth over
medium heat and keep at a gentle simmer.
Peel and de-vein the prawns.

Lightly poach eggs. Place the noodles in an
earthenware pot or cast-iron casserole and
add all the other ingredients, placing
poached eggs on top. Ladle in enough broth
to just cover the ingredients, then bring to
the boil, covered, over medium heat and
simmer for another 4-5 minutes until all the
ingredients are hot and cooked. Serve at
once in noodle bowls.

Serves 4.

—NOODLES WITH EGG BROTH—

400 g (14 oz) dried noodles (any type)
2 tablespoons cornflour
55 g (2 oz) cress or watercress
4 eggs, beaten
peeled and grated fresh root ginger, to garnish
BROTH:
1.35 litres (48 fl oz/6 cups) second dashi, page 12,
   or water and 2 teaspoons dashi-no-moto (freeze-
   dried dashi powder)
1½ teaspoons salt
4 tablespoons shoyu
1 tablespoon sugar and 2 tablespoons mirin

Cook noodles following packet instructions
and immediately wash away the starch.

In a large saucepan, mix all the ingredients
for the broth and bring to the boil. Add the
cooked noodles to the broth and when it
begins to boil again remove the noodles and
place in 4 individual noodle bowls, keeping
the broth at a gentle simmer. Dissolve the
cornflour with 4-5 tablespoons of water and
slowly add to the hot broth, stirring all the
time. The broth should be lightly thickened.

Mix the cress or watercress in the beaten
eggs in a bowl and slowly pour the mixture
over the surface of the broth. Cook for 2-3
minutes over medium heat until egg mixture
rises to the surface. Remove from the heat
and pour a quarter of the egg broth over
each of the 4 noodle bowls. Garnish with a
heap of grated root ginger and serve at once.

Serves 4.

—SOBA WITH DIPPING SAUCE—

450 g (1 lb) dried soba (buckwheat) noodles
1 sheet of nori (wafer-thin dried seaweed)
3-4 teaspoons wasabi paste or powder
2 spring onions, finely chopped
DIPPING SAUCE:
500 ml (16 fl oz/2 cups) second dashi, page 12, or
   water and 1 teaspoon dashi-no-moto (freeze-dried
   dashi powder)
115 ml (4 fl oz/½ cup) shoyu
4 tablespoons mirin
1 teaspoon sugar

Cook the noodles in plenty of boiling water, following packet instructions. Wash away the starch under running water and drain.

Lightly toast both sides of nori sheet over low heat and crush into pieces in absorbent kitchen paper or cut into 2.5 cm (1 in) long shreds with kitchen scissors. If using wasabi powder, make a paste by mixing it with the same amount of water. Mix the ingredients for dipping sauce in a saucepan and simmer over medium heat until sugar has dissolved. Half fill 4 small individual bowls or tea cups with the sauce and put the remaining sauce in a jug.

Refresh the noodles under cold running water for a second and arrange a quarter on each of 4 individual bamboo mats placed on large plates, or directly onto plates. Sprinkle the nori on top. Serve with small plates of the chopped spring onion and wasabi paste and the sauce. Diners dip some noodles into their own sauce mixed with the condiments.

Serves 4.

Note: Soba noodles can be made like udon, see page 86, using buckwheat flour.

—SHOYU RAMEN WITH PORK—

500 g (1 lb 2 oz) Chinese style egg noodles
250 g (9 oz) pork, shredded
85 ml (3 fl oz/⅓ cup) shoyu
3 tablespoons sake
85 g (3 oz) fine green beans, trimmed
200 g (7 oz) bean sprouts, trimmed
vegetable oil for frying
salt and freshly ground pepper
chilli oil, optional
BROTH:
2.5 cm (1 in) piece fresh root ginger, peeled
2 cloves garlic
2 spring onions
1.35 litres (48 fl oz/6 cups) chicken stock
2 teaspoons salt

To make broth, roughly chop root ginger, garlic and spring onions and add to chicken stock. Bring to the boil over medium heat and simmer, half-covered, for 30 minutes. Meanwhile, cook the noodles in plenty of boiling water, following packet instructions. Wash away the starch and drain. Sprinkle 1 tablespoon sake and 2 tablespoons shoyu over pork and set aside. Cut beans in half, parboil, then drain. Stir-fry bean sprouts in a little oil over high heat for 1 minute. Add beans and stir-fry for 1-2 minutes. Season with salt and pepper and remove to a plate.

Add pork to pan and stir-fry for 5-6 minutes until well cooked. Strain broth into another pan, discarding ginger, garlic and spring onions. Season with remaining shoyu and sake, salt and pepper. Bring to the boil, add the noodles and cook over medium heat for 1 minute. Divide the noodles between 4 individual noodle bowls, keeping broth at a gentle simmer. Divide cooked ingredients between bowls. Pour broth over them and serve garnished with chilli oil, if wished.

Serves 4.

SEAFOOD RAMEN

4 fresh or dried shiitake mushrooms
sugar and shoyu
vegetable oil for frying
500 g (1 lb 2 oz) Chinese style egg noodles
4 tablespoons dried cut wakame (young seaweed)
12-20 cooked peeled prawns
spring onion, shredded, to garnish
BROTH:
1.35 litres (48 fl oz/6 cups) chicken stock
2.5 cm (1 in) piece fresh root ginger, peeled and
    sliced
2 cloves garlic, sliced in half
2 spring onions, halved lengthways
3 tablespoons shoyu and 2 tablespoons sake
2 teaspoons salt
freshly ground black pepper

If using dried shiitake, soak in warm water
with a pinch of sugar for 1 hour. Meanwhile,
make broth. Put chicken stock in a pan with
ginger, garlic and spring onions, bring to the
boil and simmer, half-covered, over medium
heat for 30 minutes. Drain shiitake, discard
stalks and cut the caps into 0.5 cm (¼ in)
thick shreds. Stir-fry in a little oil for 2-3
minutes and sprinkle with a little shoyu.
Cook noodles following packet instructions;
wash off the starch. Soak the wakame in
water for 10 minutes, blanch in boiling
water for 1 minute and drain.

Strain broth into another pan, discarding
ginger, garlic and spring onions. Season with
the 3 tablespoons shoyu, 2 tablespoons sake,
the salt and a pinch of pepper. Bring to the
boil and add noodles. Cook over medium
heat for 1 minute, then transfer noodles to 4
individual noodle bowls, keeping the broth
at a gentle simmer. Spoon prawns, wakame
and mushrooms onto the noodles. Pour the
broth over the top and serve hot, garnished
with shredded spring onion.

Serves 4.

—MISO RAMEN WITH CHICKEN—

2 chicken breast fillets, skinned
2.5 cm (1 in) piece fresh root ginger, peeled and
    grated, and 3-4 tablespoons shoyu
500 g (1 lb 2 oz) Chinese style egg noodles
200 g (7 oz) bean sprouts, trimmed
vegetable oil for frying
salt and freshly ground black pepper
8 tablespoons cooked sweetcorn kernels
150 g (5 oz) spinach, trimmed
BROTH:
1.35 litres (48 fl oz/6 cups) chicken stock
2.5 cm (1 in) piece fresh root ginger, peeled and
    roughly sliced
2 cloves garlic and 2 spring onions, cut into 3 pieces
8 tablespoons miso (white, if available)
2 tablespoons each shoyu and sake

To make broth, put stock in a saucepan with
sliced ginger, garlic and spring onions. Bring
to boil and simmer over medium heat for 30
minutes. Slice chicken into 0.5 cm (¼ in)
thick, bite-size pieces. Spread pieces on a
large plate, pour over grated ginger and the
3-4 tablespoons shoyu and leave to marinate
for 10 minutes. Cook the noodles following
packet instructions and wash off any starch.
Stir-fry bean sprouts in a little oil for 1-2
minutes, season with salt and pepper and
remove to a plate. Drain chicken and fry in
a little oil until all sides are golden brown.

Blanch corn in boiling water for 1 minute;
drain. Cook spinach in lightly salted water
for 1-2 minutes, drain, squeeze out water and
cut into 2.5 cm (1 in) pieces. Strain broth
into a large pan, discarding ginger, garlic and
onions. Bring to boil. Add the 2 tablespoons
shoyu and sake and the miso diluted with a
little broth. Add noodles, bring broth to boil
and simmer for 2 minutes. Remove noodles
to 4 individual bowls, put rest of ingredients
on top and pour over the hot broth.

Serves 4.

KANTEN YOKAN

one 5 g stick dried kanten (agar-agar)
50 g (1⅔ oz) sugar
500 g (18 oz) sweet azuki (red bean) paste

Rinse the kanten with water and break into
several pieces. Soak in plenty of water for at
least 30 minutes until soft, then squeeze out
the water and tear the kanten into small
pieces. Place the kanten in a saucepan with
500 ml (18 fl oz/2¼ cups) water and cook
over moderate heat until it has dissolved. Do
not stir before this point.

Cook gently, stirring, for another 5 minutes,
then strain. Return the kanten liquid to the
pan and add the sugar. Cook over low heat,
stirring continuously, until the sugar has
dissolved and add the sweet azuki (red bean)
paste. Mix well and bring to the boil over
high heat for 3 minutes, stirring all the time.
Remove from the heat, place the pan over a
larger bowl of cold water and continue to stir
until mixture begins to thicken.

Pour mixture into a slightly wet 15 cm (6 in)
square mould or baking tin, or individual
dessert bowls, leave to cool, then place in
the refrigerator and leave to chill overnight.
Cut the kanten yokan into oblong blocks
and arrange on a green leaf on individual
plates. Serve still chilled.

Serves 6-8.

Note: Sweet azuki (red bean) paste is sold in
cans or in powdered form at oriental shops.

— FRUIT SALAD WITH KANTEN —

half 5 g stick dried kanten (agar-agar)
15 g (½ oz) sugar
1 small red apple, cut into 6 wedges and cored
salt
300 g (10 oz) can peeled tangerines or satsumas,
    syrup reserved
4 canned pear quarters, sliced in half
20 green grapes, cut in half and deseeded
strawberries, hulled, to decorate
single cream and 115 g (4 oz) sweet azuki (red
    bean) paste for serving
SYRUP DRESSING:
4-5 tablespoons pouring sugar syrup
250 ml (9 fl oz/1 cup) syrup from the canned
    tangerines or satsumas

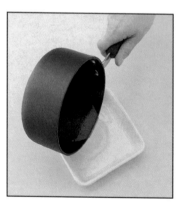

Rinse the kanten and soak it in water for
30-60 minutes, then squeeze out the water
and tear the kanten into small pieces. Put in
a saucepan with 200 ml (7 fl oz/scant 1 cup)
water and cook over moderate heat until
kanten has dissolved. Stir in the sugar and,
when it has dissolved, strain. Put the liquid
back into the pan and continue to cook,
stirring, for another 3 minutes. Pour into a
wet square mould, leave to cool, then chill
in the refrigerator. To make the dressing,
dissolve the sugar syrup in the tangerine or
satsuma syrup and chill in the refrigerator.

Slice apple wedges into thin half-open fan-
shaped pieces and plunge into salted water
to prevent discolouring. Drain and pat dry.
Cut hardened kanten into 1.5 cm (⅔ in)
dice. Put all fruits and kanten in a large salad
bowl, pour syrup dressing over them and fold
in. Decorate with strawberries and serve
with cream and sweet azuki (red bean) paste.

Serves 4-6.

–PANCAKES & RED BEAN PASTE–

3 eggs, beaten
150 g (5 oz) sugar
1 tablespoon pouring sugar syrup
180 g (6 oz/1½ cups) plain flour
1 teaspoon baking powder
vegetable oil for frying
250-300 g (9-10 oz) sweet azuki (red bean) paste

In a mixing bowl, mix eggs, sugar and syrup. Using a whisk, beat until sugar has dissolved and the mixture has a smooth consistency. Add flour, a little at a time, and mix well.

Dissolve baking powder in 150 ml (5 fl oz/ ⅔ cup) water and slowly stir into the batter. Beat well. Place a small frying pan over medium heat and when hot wipe the base with oil-soaked absorbent kitchen paper. Reduce the heat to the lowest setting and slowly ladle the batter into the centre of the pan. The size of the ladle determines the size of the 'gong' pancake – it should be about 13 cm (5 in) in diameter. Cook for about 3 minutes; when bubbles appear on the surface turn it over and cook the other side for about 2 minutes. Remove to a plate.

Repeat the process of oiling and baking until the remaining batter is used up. As the pan gets hotter, gradually reduce the cooking time by 1 minute on each side. Spread about 2 tablespoons of sweet azuki (red bean) paste in the central circle of a pancake and cover with another pancake to make a 'gong'. Alternatively, make a half gong, by folding 1 pancake folded with 1 tablespoonful of the paste inside. Serve hot or cold, accompanied by Japanese green tea.

Makes 6-8 gongs or 12-16 half gongs.

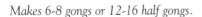

INDEX